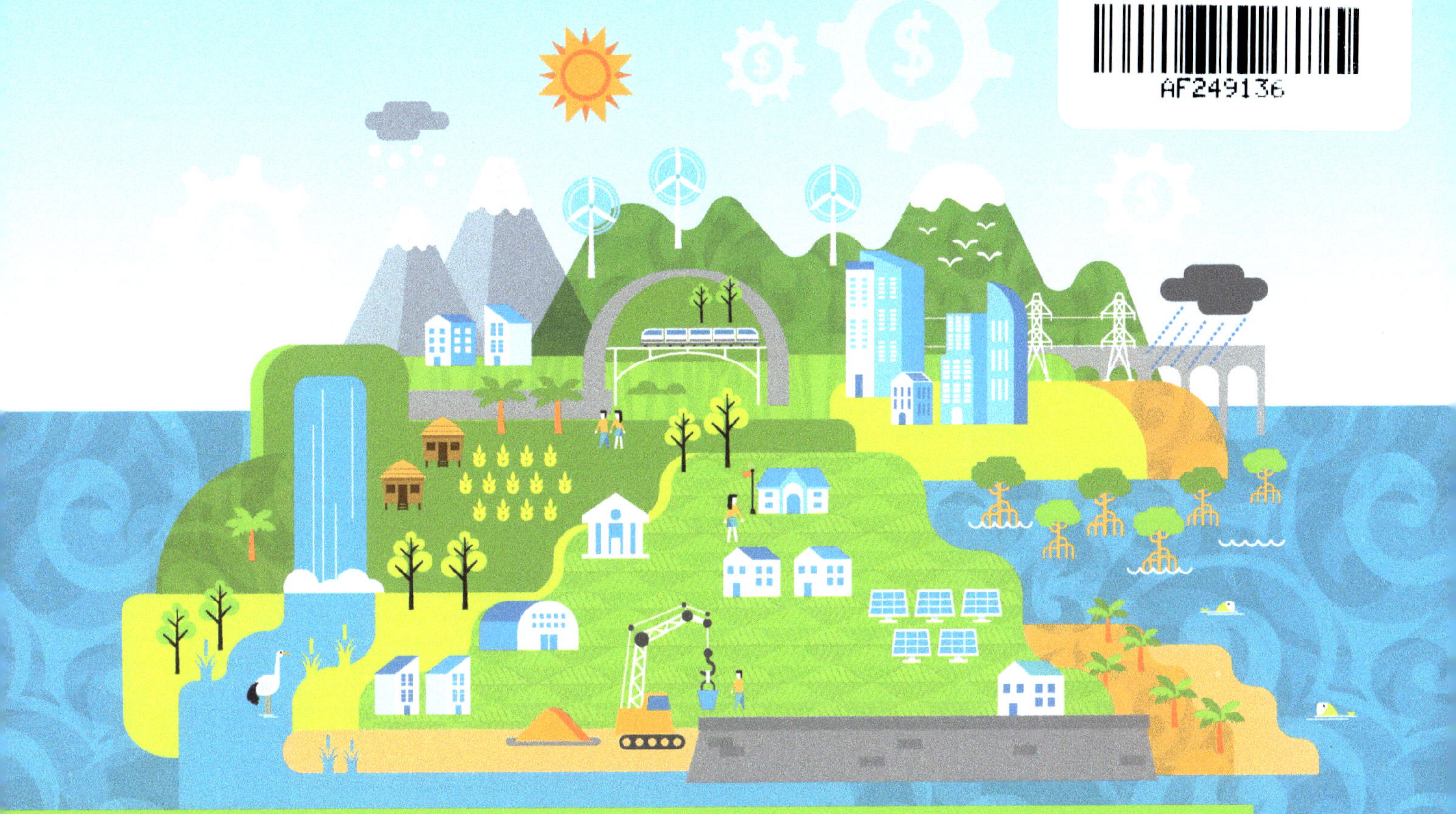

CLIMATE RESILIENT FISCAL PLANNING

A REVIEW OF GLOBAL GOOD PRACTICES

NOVEMBER 2023

ASIAN DEVELOPMENT BANK

ADB

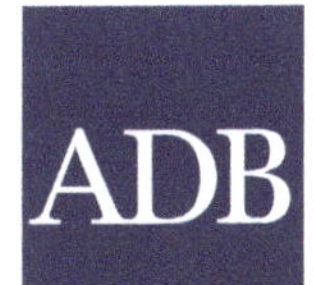

CLIMATE RESILIENT FISCAL PLANNING

A REVIEW OF GLOBAL GOOD PRACTICES

NOVEMBER 2023

ASIAN DEVELOPMENT BANK

 Creative Commons Attribution 3.0 IGO license (CC BY 3.0 IGO)

Contents

Table, Figures, and Boxes

Foreword

Central finance and planning agencies such as ministries of finance and planning and independent central banks can catalyze the scaling up of funding to tackle the effects of climate change and align spending with investments for adaptation and mitigation.

Observed and projected scenarios for global warming indicate that the adverse impacts of climate change on human and natural systems will continue to intensify across Asia and the Pacific. The World Metrological Organization suggests that global near-surface temperatures will exceed the threshold for temperature rises of 1.5°C above the preindustrial global average in at least 1 year between 2023 and 2027. The Intergovernmental Panel on Climate Change highlights that the impacts of climate change are putting ecosystems, the cryosphere, human settlements, health, food, water, and energy systems across the region at risk of breaking down.

Gaps in adaptation planning exist even as progress has been made. And at current rates of implementation, the gap between what is needed and is provided will continue to grow. Investment in adaptation will cost an estimated $215 billion–$387 billion per year for developing countries this decade according to the United Nations Environment Programme, which predicts that funding need will rise significantly over future decades toward 2050. This is in stark contrast to the $63 billion a year currently invested in adaptation globally.

Given the clear and present need to scale up spending, this report focuses on how climate resilient fiscal planning can help mobilize and allocate public and private finance for investment adaptation and resilience.

A report by the Coalition of Finance Ministers for Climate Action in 2023 outlines that finance ministries collectively control more than $30 trillion in government expenditure—which amounts to approximately one-third of global gross domestic product. These ministries coordinate economic strategy and fiscal policy and regulate the financial system. By integrating climate action into economic investments, fiscal policies, and budget management, finance ministries can help ensure economy-wide investment in adaptation. They can also deploy policy and regulation to leverage private investment in adaptation.

This report outlines evolving global good practices on climate resilient fiscal planning and identifies a three-step framework to help decision-makers scale up and align fiscal flows with investment in adaptation and resilience.

The first step is to assess climate-related fiscal risks to identify, model, and disclose the impact of climate-induced physical risks on fiscal sustainability. The second is in managing climate-related fiscal risks to guide risk assignment and risk reduction, transfer, and retention strategies. And the third step is to optimize resources to mobilize and manage public and private sources of finance for investment in adaptation.

With a focus on adaptation, this report complements the work of the Coalition of Finance Ministers for Climate Action. As an evidence-based product, it supports the Paris Agreement goal on finance and the need to scale up and align financial flows with climate adaptation.

Toru Kubo
Senior Director, Climate Change, Resilience,
  and Environment
Climate Change and Sustainable Development Department

Tariq H. Niazi
Senior Director, Public Sector Management
  and Governance Sector Office
Sectors Group

Acknowledgments

This report is a knowledge product of the Asian Development Bank (ADB) with funding support from the Climate Investment Funds Pilot Program on Climate Resilience under Regional Technical Assistance 6629: Improved Decision-Making for Climate Resilient Development in Asia and the Pacific.

The report is a result of the team effort led by Nanki Kaur, Senior Climate Change Specialist (Climate Change Adaptation), Climate Change and Sustainable Development Department (CCSD), with support from Arghya Sinha Roy, Principal Climate Change Specialist (Climate Change Adaptation), CCSD; Sugar Gonzales, Climate Change Officer (Climate Change Adaptation), CCSD; Vardan Karapetyan, Senior Project Officer, Armenia Resident Mission (ARRM), Central and West Asia Department (CWRD); Shannon Cowlin, Country Director, Mongolia Resident Mission, East Asia Department; Mohd Sani Mohd Ismail, Director, Finance Sector Office, Sectors Group (SG); Anna Fink, Senior Country Economist, Indonesia Resident Mission (IRM), Southeast Asia Department (SERD); Joao Pedro Farinha, Principal Financial Sector Economist, SG; Laisiasa Tora, Senior Public Management Specialist, SG; Ghia Rabanal, Associate Climate Change Officer, CCSD; and Anand Babu Prakasam, Project Coordinator. The report benefited from the review and feedback from Anjum Israr, Senior Public Management Specialist (Domestic Resource Mobilization), SG. Guidance was also received from Bruno Carrasco, Director General, CCSD; Toru Kubo, Senior Director, Climate Change, Resilience, and Environment, CCSD; Tariq Niazi, Senior Director, Public Sector Management and Governance Sector Office, SG; Noelle O'Brien, Director, Climate Change, CCSD; Jiro Tominaga, Country Director, IRM, SERD; Don Lambert, Country Director, ARRM, CWRD; and Emiliano Bolongaita, Principal Knowledge Specialist (Innovation), CCSD.

The report draws on multiple sources, including research and analysis from Vivid Economics, led by Oliver Walker and Elsa Kyander, with Caroline Vexler, Neil Frank, and Sarah Lewis. It benefited significantly from inputs by technical experts, including Michael Alan Schur, David Corderi-Novoa, and Stuart Anthony Kiem. The ADB team is grateful for the contributions of national consultants Davit Manukyan and Vardan Melikyan in Armenia; Putra Dwitama and Rahmad Tantawi in Indonesia; and Choikhand Janchivlamdan, Munkhzul Chimid-Ochir, and Batkhuyag Choijiljav in Mongolia. The conclusions and recommendations in this report do not necessarily reflect the views of any contributors.

ADB extends thanks to national government ministries: Ministry of Finance and Ministry of Economy of the Government of Armenia; Centre for Climate Finance and Multilateral Policy, the Fiscal Policy Agency, Ministry of Finance, Ministry of Agriculture, and Planning Bureau of the Government of Indonesia; and the Ministry of Environment and Tourism, Ministry of Economy and Development, Ministry of Finance, and Water Authority of the Government of Mongolia.

Special thanks go to national government focal points for giving their valuable time and insights: Avag Avanesyan, Deputy Minister of Finance, Government of Armenia; Zenitha Astra Paramitha, Fiscal Policy Analyst at the Centre for Climate Finance and Multilateral Policy, Fiscal Policy Agency, Ministry of Finance, Government of Indonesia; Tserendulam Shagdarsuren, Director General of the Climate Change and Policy Planning Department, Ministry of Environment and Tourism, Government of Mongolia; and Enkhmunkh Otgontogtokh, Senior Specialist (Integrated Sectoral Policy Division) in the Integrated Policy and Planning Department, Ministry of Economy and Development, Government of Mongolia.

ADB would also like to express gratitude to Lorie Rufo, former PPCR Coordinator for Climate Investment Funds. Lucy Michaela Southwood and James Unwin edited the report, while Anna Liza Cinco, Senior Operations Assistant, CCSD, provided administrative support. Ailen Marylou Bigay coordinated publication, Rocilyn Locsin Laccay designed the cover and infographics, and Edith Creus finalized the layout and composition.

Abbreviations

ADB	–	Asian Development Bank
CBA	–	cost-benefit analysis
CFA	–	central finance agencies
DGR	–	Risk Management Division (Peru)
FSM	–	Federated States of Micronesia
GDP	–	gross domestic product
IAM	–	integrated assessment model
IMF	–	International Monetary Fund
Lao PDR	–	Lao People's Democratic Republic
MCA	–	multicriteria assessment
NAP	–	national adaptation plan
PDNA	–	post-disaster needs assessment
PFM	–	public financial management
PIM	–	public investment management
PPP	–	public–private partnership
RCP	–	Representative Concentration Pathway
SDG	–	Sustainable Development Goal
SOE	–	state-owned enterprise
UK	–	United Kingdom
US	–	United States

Executive Summary

Climate-related physical risks are a significant and growing threat to fiscal sustainability. Acute and chronic physical climate-related risks—such as changing precipitation patterns, rising temperatures, and floods—are increasing in severity and frequency. These can damage infrastructure, displace vulnerable populations, disrupt economies, and require significant investments to build resilience. As a result, climate-related risks can make it very difficult for central finance agencies (CFAs) to carry out planned expenditures and meet development priorities.

CFAs urgently need to systematically incorporate climate considerations in all fiscal decision-making. CFAs can take the lead in building fiscal and economic resilience to climate change. Effective action is predicated on deep understanding of how climate-related risks affect the economy, vulnerable groups, infrastructure, and fiscal outcomes. Using this information, CFAs can build fiscal resilience to climate-related risks by developing a strategy for managing fiscal exposure and mobilizing enough resources for adaptation needs.

Many CFAs are building increasingly comprehensive approaches to deal with climate-related risks in the short and long terms.[1] They use a variety of approaches, models, and policy actions to manage and adapt to current and future climate risks. While deploying these in various ways, depending on needs and capacities, good practice approaches tend to be:

- **Evidence-driven:** Strategies, policies, and priorities are underpinned by a robust and clear understanding of how climate-related risks affect the economy and fiscal health.
- **Cost-effective:** Since public resources are increasingly limited, it is important to find cost-effective and high impact approaches to managing and adapting to climate-related risks.
- **Forward-looking and dynamic:** Climate risks require planning for uncertainty using flexible approaches that can account for multiple scenarios and adapt to new information.
- **Coordinated and collaborative:** Leveraging the knowledge of ministries, nongovernmental organizations, and the private sector can help ensure consistency in priorities and approaches to head off climate-related risks.
- **Addressing barriers:** Using innovative instruments and policy incentives can encourage investment in risk management in the short and long terms, de-risk private sector financing, and address barriers to mobilizing resources at scale.

CFAs may face challenges in integrating climate-related risk information into decision-making and in mobilizing resources for adaptation in a systematic and efficient manner. Assessing climate risks often involves highly technical modeling. In many countries, CFAs are already resource-constrained and lack capacity to undertake assessments. With many government agencies involved in designing and implementing climate-related policies, collaboration is vital to ensure coherence between priorities and to mobilize sufficient public and private resources.

This report details these good practice approaches and provides actionable insights for CFAs around the world to use climate-related risk information in making decisions.

---

[1] Examples include Armenia, Indonesia, the Philippines, and the United States. Case studies on these and other countries are included in this report.

1 Context of Fiscal Planning for Climate Risks

Climate-related risks pose a frequent, sizeable, and increasing risk to fiscal sustainability. Between 1950 and 2015, 40 countries experienced disasters that caused damage exceeding 10% of GDP (Cevik and Huang 2018).[1] In 2017, global losses related to climate change amounted to $340 billion, of which $200 were uninsured (IMF 2019a). As climate change risks increase, countries that are particularly vulnerable face persistent uncertainty over both current and future implications for fiscal sustainability.

Central finance agencies (CFAs) can play a key role in supporting national economic priorities, including priorities affected by climate change. CFAs[2] are responsible for managing public resources and can contribute to long-term economic growth by using well-designed fiscal policy to create macroeconomic stability and influence work and investment incentives (Figure 1.1; Allen et al. 2015; IMF 2015). As a result, CFAs—along with other

PPP = public–private partnership, SOE = state-owned enterprise.

Note: The International Monetary Fund (IMF) identifies a wide range of government activities and policy responsibilities of the ministry of finance or other central finance agencies (Allen et al. 2015). Based on these activities, this report defines five core central finance agency functions that work in close coordination.

Sources: Allen, R., Y. Hurcan, M. Queyranne, and S. Ylaoutinen. 2015. The Evolving Functions and Organization of Finance Ministries. *IMF Working Paper*, 15/232. Washington, DC.: International Monetary Fund; IMF. 1999. *Guidelines for Public Expenditure Management*; IMF. 2001. *Guidelines for Public Debt Management*; I. Lienert. 2010. *Optimal Structures for Ministries of Finance. Public Financial Management*, Blog, 29 March; OECD. 2013a. *Government at a Glance 2013*. Paris: OECD Publishing; Quintyn, M. and M.W. Taylor. 2004. Should Financial Sector Regulators Be Independent? Economic Issues, 32; Treasury Committee. 2011. *Principles of Tax Policy*. London: The Stationery Office Limited.

---

[1] Although many (but not all) physical hazard-driven disasters are related to climate, climate change is not always the underlying driver of individual extreme weather events, even when the risks are linked to climate change.

[2] The entity or entities responsible for government financial functions are sometimes referred to as CFA (Allen et al. 2015; World Bank 2013). The CFA is usually the ministry of finance, but can also be other ministries and agencies such as planning ministries or central banks. To reflect that the organizational structure varies across countries, this report uses the term CFA to define the government's core financial functions.

relevant institutions, such as central banks and revenue boards—can play a central role in building resilience to climate change and managing risks (Coalition of Finance Ministries for Climate Action 2022).

Acute climate-related risks such as floods and droughts and chronic risks such as changes in precipitation patterns can directly and indirectly affect public fiscal health through four main channels. These can be related and reinforcing. For example, while infrastructure damage can affect the economy by reducing the ease of trade, it can also trigger explicit liabilities. Risks can also have wider implications for debt, tax revenues, external financing needs, credit risk, and other significant indicators of fiscal health (OECD and World Bank 2019). The four impact channels listed here and outlined in Figure 1.2 are not an exhaustive list of climate-related impacts that could affect fiscal sustainability and economic development. Rather, they represent the four areas that are likely to be most relevant to CFAs and can be reasonably quantified with climate risk information.

- **Macroeconomic shocks:** The macroeconomic consequences of climate-related risks can include short-term, knock-on economic impacts and longer-term effects cascading from increased poverty, reduced investment, or strains on public resources. For example, a severe drought may directly reduce agriculture outputs and indirectly reduce output in downstream sectors that require commodities for production. Chronic climate-related risks, such as changing precipitation patterns, may also affect the productivity of highly exposed sectors, impacting household incomes and productivity in the wider economy. This can lead to government revenue losses and additional spending requirements through automatic stabilizers, which in turn can undermine the government's ability to finance external debts. Less developed countries with economies that rely on highly exposed sectors such as agriculture and fishing are expected to disproportionately experience global macroeconomic shocks from climate-related risks. Recent estimates of the economic consequences of climate-related risks to agriculture amount to 2.5%–2.9% of GDP in India and 0.8%–1.8% of GDP in Africa (Dellink, Lanzi, and Chateau 2019), rising more broadly across all sectors to as much as 27% of GDP in Asia and 37% of GDP in the Association of Southeast Asian Nations (Swiss Re Institute 2021).

- **Implicit/explicit liabilities:** Government liabilities can affect expenditures, such as relief payments to affected populations in the aftermath of a disaster and spending on infrastructure repair, or revenues due to business interruptions. This can include implicit or explicit liabilities from affected state-owned enterprises (SOEs) or public–private partnerships (PPPs), and implicit liabilities from bank failures. For example, the Government of India has increased spending on weather-based crop insurance schemes to compensate farmers against risks (Swain 2014).

- **Adaptation needs:** The costs of adapting to climate-related risks are typically highest in countries with the lowest public resources. In some developing countries, adaptation needs represent as much as 1% of GDP (Aligishiev, Massetti, and Bellon 2022), with annual adaption costs estimated at $140 billion–$300 billion by 2030 and $280 billion–$500 billion by 2050 (UNEP 2021). The private sector will have a crucial role in meeting adaptation finance needs, which at present come predominantly from public sources. And while these needs may put pressure on public resources, adaptation investments may also generate economic and fiscal benefits, reducing some areas of climate-related fiscal risk and in some cases, generating new revenue streams (Tall et al. 2021).

- **Public services:** Physical climate-related risks can lead to higher expenditure on services such as public health as a changing climate can, for example, increase the prevalence of infectious diseases, inadequate nutrition due to agriculture shocks, and mortality from extreme weather events (Ebi, Hess, and Watkiss 2017). Social protection scheme costs might also increase, as climate-related risks can lead to rising poverty rates (Tenzing 2020).

CFAs can take a lead role in managing climate-related risk and attracting enough finance flows to support fiscal sustainability and long-term development needs. The four channels of impact shown in Figure 1.2 can affect CFAs' ability to maintain fiscal sustainability and meet economic priorities. But they can use their influence on economic and fiscal policy to build fiscal and economic resilience to climate change over the short and long term, supporting fiscal resilience to climate-related risks through risk management and financing, by developing

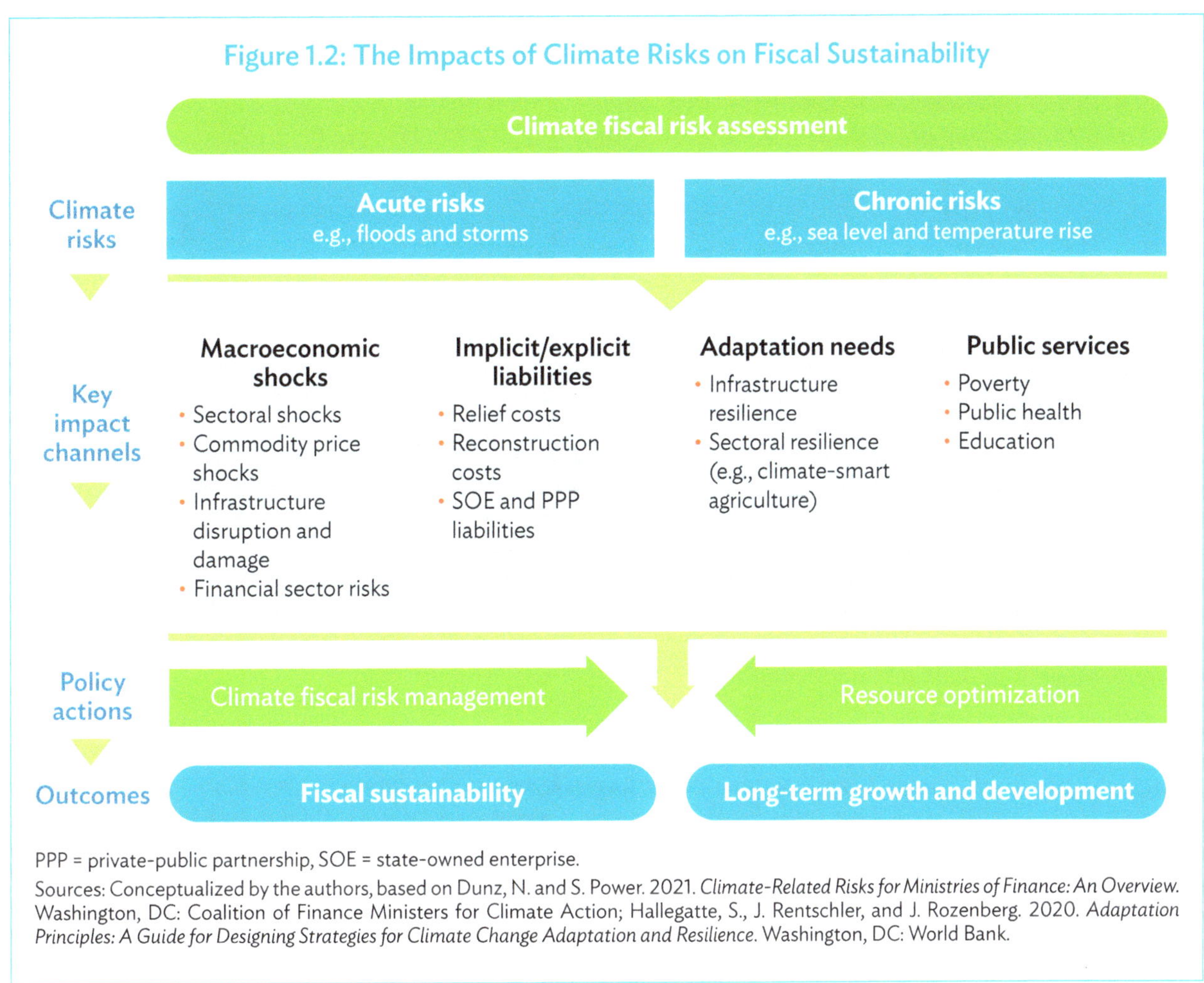

Figure 1.2: The Impacts of Climate Risks on Fiscal Sustainability

PPP = private-public partnership, SOE = state-owned enterprise.
Sources: Conceptualized by the authors, based on Dunz, N. and S. Power. 2021. *Climate-Related Risks for Ministries of Finance: An Overview.* Washington, DC: Coalition of Finance Ministers for Climate Action; Hallegatte, S., J. Rentschler, and J. Rozenberg. 2020. *Adaptation Principles: A Guide for Designing Strategies for Climate Change Adaptation and Resilience.* Washington, DC: World Bank.

a strategy for managing fiscal exposure to acute risks, and resource optimization, by mobilizing enough resources to reduce the impacts of increasing chronic and acute risks through adaptation (Coalition of Finance Ministers for Climate Action 2022).

Making internally consistent and evidence-based policies for managing climate-related risks and supporting adaptation needs is another important role. A wide body of literature on greening fiscal policy highlights several challenges CFAs face, including:

- **Incoherence between priorities:** Since many government agencies are involved in designing and implementing climate-related policies, failure to collaborate closely can create dissonance between adaptation priorities and risk modeling approaches.

- **Limited institutional capacity:** Assessing physical climate-related risks often involves conducting or using results from technical modeling. CFAs in many countries are already resource-constrained and may lack the capacity to undertake such assessments.

- **Disconnection between theory and practice:** There is a large body of guidance on greening fiscal policy and incorporating climate-related risk information into management strategies. However, much of this is theoretical, and good practices can focus on advanced policy. As such, CFA needs may not align with these approaches.

Report Structure and Objectives

The objective of this report is to provide actionable insights for CFAs on incorporating climate-related risk information into their decisions. There are three central aims. The first is to consolidate a large evidence base of resources that may be relevant to CFAs on good practices for climate risk-driven fiscal policy. Second, the report aims to make strong links between theoretical good practice and practical implementation needs, identifying entry points for good practice use of risk information in the public finance management (PFM) cycle and fiscal policy. The third aim is to consider CFA needs, objectives, and capacities, recognizing that good practice may vary across countries due to differences in human, technical, and financial capacities. More advanced approaches typically involve deeper systematic understanding of risk narratives and priorities, leveraging robust modeling approaches to account for a wide variety of risks and impacts, using risk information to guide decisions and policy tools that meet risk and adaptation needs and are fit for purpose.

The report is structured around three areas vital for integrating climate risk information into policies that build and maintain fiscal sustainability. First, CFAs can develop information on fiscal health in the context climate change, including exposure to risk and fiscal space for adaptation, by *assessing climate impacts on fiscal sustainability*. Second, CFAs can improve the effectiveness of risk management strategies by *managing climate-related fiscal risk exposures, incorporating climate-specific information and needs*. And third, *mobilizing finance for investment in climate change adaptation* can help CFAs efficiently and effectively mobilize resources for priority climate-related risks. These three fiscal policy areas overlap, and good practice often involves a consistent approach and priorities.

Each chapter is structured around actions that CFAs can deploy. Outlining two or three main approaches for incorporating climate-related risk information, the chapters detail methods for how such information can be used, discussing indispensable elements of good practice approaches, models, and methodologies that CFAs can apply in developing their own approaches, along with specific actions for fiscal policy or decision-making and case studies illustrating how countries have put these approaches into practice in different contexts. Every chapter ends with a box featuring key resources for CFA stakeholders.

Key Resources for Central Finance Agency Stakeholders

Strengthening the Role of Ministries of Finance in Driving Climate Action. A Framework and Guide for Ministers and Ministries of Finance (Coalition of Finance Ministers for Climate Action 2023): This comprehensive report provides guidance on strengthening core financial institutions for driving climate action and mainstreaming climate action across CFA functions and capabilities.

2 Climate-Related Fiscal Sustainability Assessments

CFAs can use information about climate-related risks to understand the fiscal implications of change and support evidence-based fiscal strategies. There is a wide range of approaches to choose from in assessing physical climate-related risks and resulting impacts. These vary in robustness, technical and data requirements, and information outputs.

This chapter explores good practice approaches, models, and actions that CFAs can use in climate impact assessments. The objective is to understand how evolving climate-related risks affect fiscal health through different channels, and what that implies for long-term fiscal sustainability. CFAs can break down climate impact assessments into three stages (Table 2.1):

1. **Pre-assessment:** This phase has two main aspects. The first is identifying who should be involved in the assessment (World Bank 2013). This is important to ensure a consistent view on risks and priorities across government agencies, and that assessment outputs can be mainstreamed into existing models and policy frameworks (G20 and OECD 2013). The second—identifying how the analysis outputs will be used—could include using risk information for a PFM strategy, using disclosure information in a fiscal risk statement, or integrating key indicators into revenue forecasts. Identifying these needs before undertaking a climate impact assessment can ensure that outputs are relevant to decisions.

2. **Assessment:** Impact assessments can take various forms, depending on CFA needs and objectives and available information about climate-related risks. This phase is likely to include scoping—or prioritizing material physical risks for assessment—and analysis, or leveraging climate-related risk information to assess impacts on a set of fiscal health metrics.

3. **Post-assessment:** This phase can help ensure that relevant stakeholders use the results of a climate impact assessment and that assessment approaches are sustainable. It can include integrating results into CFA modeling tools, disclosing risks for transparency, and decisions around ownership, information dissemination, and frequency of updates.

Within each phase, CFAs can undertake various approaches, models, and policy actions, depending on their needs and capacities. More robust approaches will deploy more complex analytical models, cover a wider variety of climate-related risks and impacts, test sensitivities and scenarios, and consider forward-looking implications. More advanced actions typically involve greater collaboration between stakeholders, systematic use of risk information, and transparency in disclosure.

Table 2.1: Stages of Climate Impact Assessment

Analytical steps		Key actions
Pre-assessment	**Review institutional environment**	Assess institutional capacity to deliver, integrate, and update impact assessments.
		Identify major stakeholders and potential partners to involve in the assessment.
	Coordinate data and modeling	Identify outputs the assessment must deliver to link to existing fiscal policy and modeling tools.
		Review potential data sources, including public or independent data sources, existing and/or centralized disaster or information on climate-related risk and assumptions used by other ministries.
Assessment	**Scope material risks**	Identify the main sources of climate-related risks and impacts on social, economic, and fiscal outcomes.
		Prioritize channels of impact for inclusion in the climate impact assessment.
	Assess fiscal impact	Qualitatively or quantitatively assess the direct and indirect fiscal implications of climate and disaster risk.
		Use scenario analysis or stress testing to assess resilience.
		Assess financing and fiscal vulnerability gaps.
		Identify priorities for risk management and adaptation financing.
Post-assessment	**Mainstream and disseminate findings**	Integrate findings into relevant models, policies, and institutional frameworks.
		Share findings with ministries and stakeholders and/or disclose them publicly in a fiscal risk statement.
	Determine updates and identify areas for improvement	Assign ownership over assessment maintenance and updates.
		Determine the frequency of updates.
		Identify gaps and potential areas for improvement.

Source: ADB.

Approaches to Climate Impact Assessment

Good practice approaches to assessing the fiscal implications of climate-related risks consider three fundamental dimensions. The first is *coverage of risks and impacts:* how comprehensively and robustly does it assess direct and indirect climate-related risks and adaptation impacts? This includes identifying climate-related risks and quantifying risks using metrics such as the external debt-to-GDP ratio, short-term external debt ratio reserves, and the external debt-to-exports ratio. The second is *sensitivity and stress testing:* does it use multiple scenarios to stress test the implications of climate-related risks on public finances and indicators of fiscal health? And the third is *forward-looking implications:* does the assessment include a forward-looking view of climate-related fiscal risks? Do the scenarios include uncertainty across climate and socioeconomic futures, in a way that is consistent with global good practices for scenario analysis?

Coverage of Risks and Impacts

Good practice approaches assess key climate-related risks to public finances. Although public expenditure requirements that stem from explicit and implicit liabilities are the most salient source of climate-related fiscal risk today, as climate-related risks increase in magnitude, indirect impacts and adaptation needs may become more material. Chronic climate-related risks may affect the distribution of economic sectors, while climate-driven disasters can have significant downside macroeconomic consequences. Effects on GDP, revenue collection, and long-term expenditure needs may trigger additional borrowing needs, meaning that impact assessments limited to expenditure analysis may significantly underestimate fiscal implications.

Historical analyses, such as post-disaster needs assessments (PDNAs), can provide information on the economic impacts of climate-related risks. Although PDNAs are not specific fiscal impact assessments and lack a forward-looking perspective, the approach demonstrates a framework for determining channels of economic impact that are relevant for CFAs, as illustrated by the Lao People's Democratic Republic (Lao PDR) case study in Box 2.1. Some countries have started prioritizing macroeconomic analysis of disasters in fiscal impact assessments. For example, the United States has expanded its approach to include both physical and transition risks, alongside the impact of adaptation needs on fiscal sustainability.

Box 2.1: Using Historical Analysis: Lessons from the Lao PDR

Supported by the World Bank, the Global Facility for Disaster Reduction and Recovery, and other stakeholders, the Government of the Lao PDR led a post-disaster needs assessment (PDNA) of the impacts of climate-related risks to support resource mobilization after severe flooding. In 2018, record high rainfall led to severe flash flooding across the country, affecting more than 132,000 households. The government conducted the PDNA immediately after the flood. It aimed to streamline disaster recovery and improve post-disaster management and reconstruction plans by assessing impacts on major economic sectors and populations.

A PDNA determines the impact of a disaster by assessing the difference between economic conditions before and after a disaster. This approach focuses on impacts on sectors, their implications for future risk, and priority recovery needs. It uses sector assessments to draw implications for human development, poverty, and macroeconomic performance. After determining the economic impact, a PDNA offers a recovery strategy that prioritizes immediate humanitarian needs, economic stability, and future resilience. This requires establishing the scale of impacts around four basic areas:

- Damage to public and private infrastructure and assets, including the agriculture, tourism, commerce, industry, and finance sectors.
- Disruption of access to goods and services, including electricity, communications, community infrastructure, transport, water, sanitation, and hygiene.
- Impacts on governance and decision-making, including disaster risk reduction, environment and forestry, employment and livelihoods, social protection, gender equality, and social inclusion.
- Needs for recovery.

The Lao PDR used the estimated value of damage and losses to assess the impact of the floods on economic performance, employment, and poverty. The impact assessment showed that damage and losses had a significant impact on infrastructure-dependent sectors, with agriculture and transport most affected. Gross domestic product had declined by 2.1% and debt increased by 70%. The assessment also found substantive destruction of farms, small enterprises, and disrupted social services, which exacerbated nutrition, health, and education challenges. Gaining understanding of the channels of impact and magnitudes enabled the government to target pivotal areas of recovery in a timely manner and across geographies, with funding for social services targeted toward vulnerable households.

The PDNA relied on historical loss data and post-disaster data collection, with substantial collaboration between government agencies, private sector partners, civil society organizations, and development partners. This approach has the benefit of using real disaster information (as opposed to modeled or estimated losses), which could inform scenario analysis or stress testing of fiscal sustainability. It is possible to leverage PDNA outcomes to understand the potential implications of future disasters of similar magnitudes, which can help determine the scale of a probable worst-case climate-related risk scenario and appropriate fiscal risk management strategy.

Although historical analyses can provide relevant details of climate-related risks, they are not forward-looking. As climate-related risks evolve, historical data may not capture the changing frequency and severity of climate-related risks. So, even as a baseline for scenario analysis, PDNAs may have limited ability to analyze current and future implications of climate-related risks and their fiscal ramifications. When used in place of forward-looking analyses, incomplete baseline information can skew future impact assessments.

continued on next page

Box 2.1 *continued*

Key takeaways

- The PDNA approach demonstrates how post-disaster analysis can help determine economic impacts of climate-related risks and their relevant channels of impact in a particular geography or economy.
- PDNAs provide a robust framework for resource mobilization after a climate-related event.
- Historical analysis can be useful but provides limited forward-looking information, which may be necessary in the context of climate change.

Lao PDR = Lao People's Democratic Republic
Sources: GFDRR. 2013. *Post-Disaster Needs Assessment Guidelines and Recovery Planning, Volume A*. Global Facility for Disaster Reduction and Recovery; Government of Lao People's Democratic Republic. 2018. *Post-Disaster Needs Assessment. 2018 Floods: Lao PDR.*

CFAs can assess economywide implications by linking first order impacts—such as sector shocks or physical damage costs—to macroeconomic models. Some commonly used macroeconomic models are outlined below.

- **Dynamic input-output models:** These demand-driven models assess linkages between sectors and regions in an economy and can reflect development and adjustment over time (Basel Committee on Banking Supervision 2021; GIZ 2022). CFAs can integrate physical climate-related risks as an input into the model by using historical information on damages—such as reduced capital stock in the real estate sector, higher imports due to lower productivity, or economic losses from reduced use of transport infrastructure (GIZ 2022)—to understand how their impacts on one sector can cascade into the wider economy. While historical information may not reflect future risk conditions, particularly in the context of increasing climate-related risks, it can provide a robust evidence base for shorter-term outlooks. For longer-term outlooks, users can combine historical information with additional evidence on how risks may increase over time to develop a reasonable set of assumptions on risk profile. Koks and Thissen (2016) use this model type to assess the economic impacts of flooding in The Netherlands on the rest of Europe.

- **Computable general equilibrium models:** These models use a system of equations representing interactions between different actors (firms, households, government, etc.) within an economy and CFAs can use them to understand how shocks to one sector affect the wider economy (OECD 2021). They provide a granular assessment of the macroeconomic impacts of climate change by, for example, accounting for differences in climatic vulnerability across regions (GIZ 2021; OECD 2021). Denmark's Ministry of Finance and the associated Danish Research Institute for Economic Analysis and Modeling use these models, combined with other sector-specific ones, to assess the impact of climate risks and policies on GDP, wages, and investment (OECD 2021). Their experience highlights three main conclusions for other applications: (i) country context matters, as national differences in economic structure, policy priorities, and climate risks can cause vastly different results; (ii) cooperation and data transparency facilitate the best results; and (iii) there should be shared understanding on how insights and subsequent policy measures impact significant economic outcomes. These findings are contingent on assumptions, which may affect the model's accuracy (OECD 2021).

- **Integrated assessment models (IAMs):** These large-scale numeric models combine economic analysis with energy use, land use, and climate-related risk information into a single model (Burns, Jooste, and Schwerhoff 2021). They calibrate physical risk losses and their impact on global GDP and temperature based on sector and regional studies. Users then estimate impacts, assuming different levels of adaptation (Aligishiev, Massetti, and Bellon 2022). The cost of private adaptation is not always included in IAMs, which may overestimate the benefits of adaptation, while technological progress is also not always included either, which underestimates the potential benefits of adaptation. The net effect of these omissions is uncertain (Aligishiev, Massetti, and Bellon 2022). The RFF-CMCC European Institute on Economics and the Environment's WITCH model is an open-source IAM model that accounts for dynamic climate-related risk mitigation and adaptation across dozens of macroregions for the next 100 years (WITCHMODEL 2022).

- **Dynamic stochastic general equilibrium models:** These repeatedly simulate many random climate shocks over the long term. Such scenario analysis enables CFAs to examine how different risk management strategies can impact long-term economic development (Aligishiev, Massetti, and Bellon 2022), allowing them to identify channels through which climate shocks affect the economy, determine appropriate post-climate shock financing needs, and analyze the costs and benefits of different risk management tools. Cantelmo, Melina, and Papageorgiou (2019) use this model to determine the channels through which climate shocks affect macroeconomic outcomes in disaster-prone countries, and the authors assess the welfare loss as equivalent to a 1.6% permanent fall in consumption.

- **Threshold 21 model:** This computer-based sustainable development analysis tool is designed to evaluate a country's development by linking environment, economic, and social factors into one tool (Millennium Institute 2015). CFAs can use it to determine suitable fiscal risk management strategies. The Government of Jamaica used this model as an analytical tool to integrate economic, social, and environmental sectors to choose long-term policy goals on land use, water demand, pollution, and energy consumption (Millennium Institute 2015).

- **Econometric models:** These models use cross-sectional analysis to estimate climate change impacts at sector and macroeconomic levels (Aligishiev, Massetti, and Bellon 2022), typically using panel data to project the short-term impact of climate shocks. Long-term assessments may be inaccurate, as these models often fail to account for adaptive behaviors. Kalkuhl and Wenz (2020) use econometric analysis to determine temperature effects on productivity levels across 77 different countries, Kahn et al. (2019) use a novel econometric approach to analyze the impact of climate change on economic growth, which disaggregates short- and long-term impacts and account for feedback loops, and IMF (2022) uses the model to quantify fiscal risks from climate change in Armenia.

CFAs can use fiscal health indicators to assess aggregate fiscal implications. A clear set of measurable fiscal health indicators can help monitor fiscal impact assessments over time and link them to fiscal priorities. Indicators can include single measurement units, such as tax revenues or financing gaps, or composite indicators for fiscal health and economic growth, such as a debt-to-GDP ratio or gross external financing requirements, which are typically expressed as: the sum of short-term external debt, amortization of medium- and long-term external debt, less the current account balance (sometimes also as share of foreign exchange reserves). The Pakistan case study in Box 2.2 discusses how to estimate indicators such as annual expected losses from statistical assessments and use these to inform disaster risk management priorities. It is also possible to link effective indicators to fiscal priorities. For example, Brazil produces 3-year forecasts for real GDP growth, inflation, real dollar exchange rate, and short-term interest rates, to ensure budget priorities align with fiscal sustainability objectives (IMF 2018). This allows it to prioritize indicators such as gross external financing requirements over more general debt sustainability indicators, should foreign exchange reserves fall below specific targets.

Box 2.2: Using Fiscal Health Indicators: Lessons from Pakistan

The World Bank, with assistance from Pakistan's Ministry of Finance, analyzed historical disaster risk data to understand fiscal implications and risk management priorities in the country. Statistical assessments of climate-related fiscal risks require significant data on historical losses and post-disaster expenditures. The World Bank used data on disaster type, affected populations, and post-disaster expenditure from Pakistan's National and Provincial Disaster Management Authority from 1973 to 2012 to understand the frequency and severity of disasters. The assessment identified flood risks as the most prevalent hazard, affecting more than three-quarters of all disaster-impacted populations over the study period.

The assessment found that floods could lead to annual losses of up to 0.8% of gross domestic product (GDP). Data limitations meant it was only possible to conduct a robust statistical analysis for flooding. The study estimated two types of risk metric: annual expected loss, which estimates the long-term average loss, and probable maximum loss, which estimates the largest potential annual loss. Estimating these metrics at national and regional levels based on per capita loss estimates, the analysis found that annual fiscal losses range from $1.2 billion–1.8 billion (0.3%–0.8% of GDP), with 1-in-100-year events threatening upward of $15 billion (7% of GDP).

continued on next page

Box 2.2 *continued*

Understanding climate-related disaster risk enabled Pakistan to strengthen its disaster risk governance. Following this assessment, the government announced its National Disaster Risk Reduction Policy, outlining the operational development of risk reduction and risk management for different hazards. Pakistan, as part of its partnership with the Asian Development Bank, also set goals for implementing national plans to reduce disaster risks and enhance preparedness by strengthening fiscal risk management.

Statistical assessments of climate-related fiscal risks can be robust but require significant data on historical losses and post-disaster expenditures. Data availability can be a challenge in conducting statistical fiscal risk analysis. As a first step, collecting and consolidating data can help determine whether statistical assessment is an appropriate approach. Next, mainstreaming statistical analysis into regular central finance agency practices, such as the public finance management cycle, can help facilitate more robust findings and encourage greater data collection efforts among ministries. This can have the added benefit of ensuring budgeting and analysis are linked, giving a more holistic overview of exposure and risk to public finances.

Costs related to climate risks may vary—not only on the risk profile and economic impact, but also on the structure of the government's contingent liabilities. As Pakistan's fiscal risk analysis develops quantified and forward-looking analysis, it may be limited in coverage of impacts due to predefined liabilities. A government's assumed liabilities after an acute climate event depend on contracts and legislation. If the government has not defined its risk ownership, it may be politically or morally obligated to pay out implicit liabilities to minimize economic damages and to consider its non-statutory responsibilities to minimize humanitarian impacts. As such, the outcomes of a risk analysis may be imprecise if it fails to account for liability structure.

Key takeaways

- Using robust historical analysis to understand climate-related risks can help central finance agencies to make informed risk management decisions.
- Robust analysis requires robust data, which can be built up by integrating data collection into central finance agency practices.
- Modeling annual expected and probable maximum losses can be a useful fiscal health indicator to use in decision-making.
- Tailoring the results of statistical modeling to a government's specific contingent liabilities is important to ensure modeling results are accurate and relevant.

Sources: ADB and World Bank. 2021. *Climate Risk Country Profile: Pakistan*; World Bank and GFDRR. 2015. *Fiscal Disaster Risk Assessment Options for Consideration: Pakistan*. Washington, DC: World Bank Publishing.

Sensitivity and Stress Testing

Stress testing is increasingly used as an approach to address climate-related risk uncertainties and assess the resilience of public finances. Stress testing, or scenario analysis, is a well-developed process promoted and frequently used by the International Monetary Fund (IMF), World Bank, and others to assess fiscal sustainability to risks. It is increasingly promoted as an approach for assessing climate-related resilience because it allows the user to account for uncertainties and understand the implications of worst-case scenarios (Adrian, Morsink, and Schumacher 2020a). The IMF uses disaster stress testing in Small Island Developing States to assess the potential impacts of asset damages on important sectors such as tourism (Adrian, Morsink, and Schumacher 2020b). For example, it used a disaster-specific stress testing approach to assess the resilience of debt sustainability in the Federated States of Micronesia (FSM), testing the impacts of a one-off shock on debt-to-GDP ratio, real economic growth, and exports. The scenario development was informed by disaster information but did not rely on disaster risk modeling. The results demonstrated that the FSM's external debt dynamics are susceptible to shocks, finding that, under a baseline scenario with no fiscal consolidation efforts between the 2019 and 2023 fiscal years, returns to investment that are as much as 2% lower than expected in the government's trust fund could rapidly increase in external debt-to-GDP and render FSM's debt stock unsustainable (IMF 2019b). The approach demonstrates that where detailed modeling information is not available, stress testing can be simplified and built directly into existing macro fiscal tools for assessing fiscal sustainability.

Forward-Looking Implications

As risks from climate change increase, good practice approaches include a forward-looking view of how risks to public finances may evolve. Climate-related risks are typically characterized in terms of impacts from acute risks, such as floods and tropical cyclones. But over the longer term, these are likely to increase, with significant implications for economic structure and adaptation needs. Many countries are starting to develop forward-looking views on climate change in fiscal reporting; the US case study in Box 2.3 demonstrates an advanced approach to comprehensively quantifying a wide range of impacts that are increasing in severity over time.

Box 2.3: Taking a Forward-Looking View: Lessons from the United States

In 2022, the United States enhanced its federal budgeting forecasts to include the impacts of physical and transition risks from climate change. This analysis focused on integrating six areas linked to the federal budget—crop insurance, coastal disasters, health care spending, wildland fire suppression, facility flood risk, and flood insurance.[a] These were selected using three criteria: vulnerability to climate-related risks, strength of links to the federal budget, and availability of economic and scientific data to conduct quantitative impact assessments. To assess the impact of each area on the federal budget, the budget forecast used quantitative assessments based on best available evidence or conducted new analysis based on preexisting models and data.

The forecasting approach used estimates of impacts under two globally recognized climate scenarios. Representative Concentration Pathways (RCPs) describe potential physical and transition outcomes under different climate scenarios. RCP is widely used when modeling climate-related risks and is globally recognized as a prominent approach to climate modeling and scenario analysis. Two scenarios—RCP4.5 (strong climate action, lower physical impacts) and RCP8.5 (limited climate action, higher physical impacts)—are generally considered good practice for analysis to account for uncertainty and understand potential fiscal impacts in futures where transition or physical risks are high.

The analysis quantifies potential impacts on federal spending by mid- and late century. It estimates that annual federal spending will increase by $5.4 billion by 2050 under RCP4.5 and by almost $37 billion under RCP8.5. Between 2081 and 2099, estimates increase this to $25 billion for RCP4.5 and to $130 billion for RCP8.5. Costs related to coastal disasters account for the largest share of this increase; causing, on average, 84% of the estimated total increase by 2050 and 75% of expenditure by late century. But annual variation in climatic conditions means that these costs will fluctuate year-to-year, making planning and budgeting increasingly challenging. The forecast also extrapolates projected losses to estimate that a 3 degree Celsius increase in global temperature by the end of the century could lead to losses in federal revenues of 7.1%. But these figures are highly uncertain and depend on assumptions around economic losses and gross domestic product growth rates.

Linking the evidence base on fiscal risk disclosures to policy decisions is central to meeting targeted spending. The scenario analysis helps the United States government advise on budgetary actions that could mitigate identified risks. For example, it gives the Department of Agriculture's Forest Service and the Department of the Interior important information on how expenditure may rise with an increase in burnt areas from wildfires and how to budget accordingly. The assessment also provides an evidence base for new policy measures aimed at reducing climate-related fiscal risks. For example, the federal budget for 2024 introduces a proposal to incentivize farmers to plant crops with higher resilience to climate change, which could reduce the federal cost of crop insurance.

Although the assessment represents an advanced quantitative approach to gauging climate-related fiscal risks, there are further opportunities to increase robustness. First, due to data limitations, the assessment of each area differs in terms of RCPs and time periods, reducing comparability. Second, the analysis omits potentially significant risks, such as impacts on transportation, energy, and water infrastructure. And third, it does not consider adaptation investments that might reduce future fiscal costs and the report states that further work is needed to better understand the potential benefits of these actions.

continued on next page

Box 2.3 *continued*

Key takeaways

- Building forward-looking tools to quantify climate-related risks on fiscal spending can support targeted budgeting and risk management.
- Using scenario analysis can help central finance agencies quantify uncertainties and understand the range of plausible fiscal outcomes.
- Understanding the fiscal impact of investments in adaptation and mitigation is an emerging area for research and vital for developing more robust forward-looking fiscal sustainability assessments in future.

[a] Some of the six areas are crosscutting, showing that impact channels can be connected and reinforce each other. Federal facility flood risks and coastal disasters can lead to macroeconomic shocks due to infrastructure damage and disruption. Budget implications from crop insurance, flood insurance, coastal disasters, and wildfire suppression are implicit and explicit liabilities. Federal health care increases spending on public services. The assessment does not cover adaptation costs.

Sources: OECD. 2021a. *Climate Change and Long-term Fiscal Sustainability.* Paris: OECD Publishing; The White House. 2022. *Briefing Room: Quantifying Risks to the Federal Budget from Climate Change.* https://www.whitehouse.gov/omb/briefing-room/2022/04/04/quantifying-risks-to-the-federal-budget-from-climate-change/; The White House. 2023. *Briefing Room: The Importance of Measuring the Fiscal and Economic Costs of Climate Change.* https://www.whitehouse.gov/omb/briefing-room/2023/03/14/the-importance-of-measuring-the-fiscal-and-economic-costs-of-climate-change/; US Office of Management and Budget. 2022. *Climate Risk Exposure: An Assessment of the Federal Government's Financial Risks to Climate Change.*

Climate-related risk assessments should align with well-recognized assumptions around future conditions. The Representative Concentration Pathway (RCP) approach, which uses a range of assumptions around socioeconomic changes and climate policy that affect greenhouse gas emissions and climate-related risks, is most used to assess physical risks. RCPs are linked to Shared Socioeconomic Pathways, another set of well understood future scenarios around population growth, economic development, urbanization, and other societal trends. Leveraging these approaches can help account for potential uncertainties and ensure that assessment approaches are well understood and credible. The US and Armenia case studies (Boxes 2.3 and 2.4) describe the use of scenarios and RCPs, which capture a range of uncertainties around physical and transition risks.

Box 2.4: Using Climate Scenarios: Lessons from Armenia

Armenia is highly exposed to acute and chronic climate-related impacts that pose risks to the economy and society. Acute risks come from the high frequency of intensive climate-related hazards, resulting in droughts, landslides, mudflows, wildfires, and so on. Sources of chronic risk include increased average temperature, decreased precipitation, and land degradation.

Armenia has taken significant steps to develop its institutional arrangements and policies to respond to climate change-related risks. It has developed and adopted a national adaptation plan, identified vulnerable sectors, and made progress in developing sector adaptation plans. Its cross functional Inter-Agency Council on Climate Change coordinates the country's climate change response.[a]

In 2022, the Ministry of Finance started including disaster and climate risk into its fiscal risk statement. After identifying acute and chronic risks and providing a qualitative analysis on their impact on the macro fiscal environment, the ministry worked with the International Monetary Fund to quantify the risks, using an econometric model to reflect simulations in an analytical framework that links estimates of changing climate patterns on the real economy and with long-term fiscal projections. This considered: the impact of higher temperatures on the economy, based on an empirical analysis of the effect of past temperature changes on growth; how slower economic growth flows through to fiscal projections to identify building fiscal pressures; and discrete climate change-related fiscal risks—including those translated through state-owned enterprises and public–private partnerships—to identify the state's direct exposures to climate risks. To assess fiscal pressure, the study focused on fiscal health and economic growth indicators, such as gross domestic product (GDP), public expenditures, net borrowing, and debt-to-GDP ratio.

continued on next page

Box 2.4 *continued*

The study developed three scenarios relative to the baseline, which projected the long-term fiscal situation based on current policies in the absence of climate change. These were:

- **The Paris Agreement scenario,** where the country meets its international commitments under the agreement. In this scenario, GDP remains unchanged from the baseline, and public debt is 46% of GDP by 2072.
- **The unmitigated scenario**, where global greenhouse gas emissions continue to increase throughout the century, leading to a temperature increase of about 5.5 degree Celsius over average 1990s levels by 2090–2100. Under this scenario, public debt levels could reach 62% of GDP if there is no fiscal policy response. Interestingly, investing in adaptation can reduce the fiscal impact, even in the unmitigated scenario, and reduce public debt from 62% to 54% of GDP by 2072.
- **The volatile scenario**, which takes the unmitigated scenario and adds the higher volatility of weather and more extreme weather events. Under this scenario, climate change impacts could reduce GDP per capita by 18% relative to the baseline by 2072, and in the absence of any fiscal policy response, public debt levels could reach an unsustainable 140% of GDP.

The next step—a sector-level analysis—is crucial for translating physical and macro understanding of climate risks into a sector-by-sector understanding to inform risk management, including adaptation plans and investment planning. Undertaking this level of analysis will give the government a stronger evidence base on how, where, and how much to respond, allowing it to balance the many competing demands on limited fiscal space.

Key takeaways

- Having access to historical climate-related risks data and robust tools for analysis enables central finance agencies to quantify macro fiscal implications.
- Understanding the risks of implicit liabilities on the state balance translated through state-owned enterprises and public–private partnerships gives central finance agencies a holistic picture of risks.
- Sector-level climate change-related fiscal risks assessments allow central finance agencies to target risk management and allocate resources.

[a] Decree N 719-A of the Prime Minister of the Republic of Armenia on 6 July 2021.
Sources: IMF. 2022. *Armenia: Technical Report—Quantifying Fiscal Risks from Climate Change*; Kahn, M.E., K. Mohaddes, R. N. C. Ng, M. H. Pesaran, M. Raissi, and J. C. Yang. 2019. Long-Term Macroeconomic Effects of Climate Change: A Cross-country Analysis. *IMF Working Paper*, 19/215. Washington, DC: International Monetary Fund; Republic of Armenia. 2021. *National Adaptation Plan*. https://unfccc.int/sites/default/files/resource/NAP_Armenia.pdf.

Approaches for Embedding Climate-Related Impact Assessments

Post-assessment, CFAs can take three essential actions to help ensure fiscal sustainability information is broadly available and widely used. First, they can disclose climate risk assessments findings to the public, along with the important implications and actions to reduce adverse impacts on the fiscal position. Second, they can integrate and embed the impacts of climate-related risks in their modeling tools. And third (as discussed in the next two chapters), they can embed the results of fiscal sustainability assessments in policy and practice to guide fiscal policy decisions and actions.

Public Disclosure

Publicly disclosing climate-related risks is an important good practice in fiscal impact assessment. The benefits and processes are similar to those from disclosing other sources of fiscal risk. An important benefit includes ensuring that CFAs consider climate-related risks within a broader suite of systemic risks and manage them alongside other priority fiscal risks. Robust analysis, management strategy, and disclosure of climate-related fiscal risks can also help underpin creditworthiness and improve market confidence.

The IMF and other prominent international institutions recommend that climate-related fiscal risks are included in wider fiscal risk disclosures, with quantitative information on their magnitude and implications (IMF 2018). The Philippines publishes an annual fiscal risk statement that includes a section on the impacts of human-induced disasters and disasters triggered by natural hazards, with estimates of the economic impact of disasters focused on damage to assets, the most affected sectors, and investment needs. It also considers short-term, forward-looking risk implications based on the El Niño cycle.[3] Where relevant, the fiscal risk statement refers to ongoing management and funding initiatives to address the physical and economic implications of recent disasters. It also includes suggested reforms and efforts to improve fiscal risk management, which relevant authorities can use to amend fiscal practices in the PFM cycle (Development Budget Coordination Committee 2021).

Model Integration

Integrating climate-related risk information into existing CFA modeling tools can also contribute to more comprehensive and coordinated fiscal risk management. There are two main benefits of using data on climate-related risks in modeling tools. First, it can help CFAs to identify the primary and secondary impacts of climate-related risks on key economic variables, such as GDP, employment, and adaptation financing needs (GIZ 2021; World Bank 2022). Second, it can support a consistent view of climate-related risk across ministries that rely on modeling outputs, facilitating coordination and inter-ministerial cooperation (GIZ 2021). The case study on Mexico's system for developing and disseminating risk information (Box 2.5) illustrates the importance of close coordination for effective risk management and responsiveness.

Box 2.5: Developing and Disseminating Risk Information: Lessons from Mexico

Mexico is highly exposed to a range of climate-related hazards—particularly storms, flooding, and drought—which pose risks to the economy and vulnerable groups. About 40% of its land area and nearly one-third of its population are estimated to be at risk from physical hazards, and more than 70% of economic activity is exposed to at least two hazards.

To address its endemic exposure to climate-related risks and other physical hazards, Mexico has developed a robust evidence-based disaster risk management system. The government established the National System for Civil Protection (SINAPROC) in close coordination with line ministries and other stakeholders, providing an overarching disaster risk management system that can help identify, prevent, and finance risk and manage reconstruction. The National Disaster Prevention Centre (CENAPRED)—which provides technical development support within SINAPROC—works closely with academia and the scientific sector to develop robust and consistent data. Sectors, line ministries, and state and municipal governments are responsible for gathering scientific and other hazard-exposure data for the hazard databases. This includes detailed information on demographics and infrastructure exposure.

SINAPROC uses spatially granular risk atlases to communicate risk information and inform decision-making at various levels. CENAPRED has developed risk atlases that show hazards, population, and infrastructure risk exposure at national, state, and local levels. Although these are used mainly for emergency response planning, they are available for public use to raise risk awareness. This approach demonstrates good practice for making consistent risk information available as part of disaster risk management strategies and helps identify the main hazards early.

Institutional coordination between national and subnational governments could help improve risk responses. Mexico's decentralized government is split between federal, provincial, and municipal systems. This can lead to a siloed approach, with insufficient communication between subnational governments and specialized federal agencies. This was demonstrated in September 2017, when two earthquakes hit the states of Puebla, Morelos, Guerrero, and Oaxaca and a lack

continued on next page

---

[3] El Niño is a weather phenomenon lasting 9–12 months on average and occurring every 2 to 7 years. It leads to changes in the direction and strength of winds over the Pacific Ocean around the equator, causing above-average temperatures over the central and eastern Pacific Ocean. This, in turn, leads to abnormal precipitation patterns, particularly south of the equator (World Bank 2015).

Box 2.5 *continued*

of communication between government organizations led to a slow and inadequate response. And while earthquakes are not driven by climate, the impacts on assets and populations can be similar, demonstrating that streamlined communication after a climate event can help governments meet relief and recovery needs more efficiently.

Stakeholders have noted that clearer delineation of responsibilities would help strengthen coordination. Although SINAPROC uses detailed models to map flood-prone areas, there is room to bolster their management of community-level risk assessments, especially where vulnerable population conditions are present. Improving intragovernmental communication could help ensure valuable data on climate-related risks are shared between national government agencies. Sharing this information can also help governments reduce risks when investing in development projects and help ensure, for example, that municipal governments consider climate-related risk exposure and take actions to reduce risks where applicable when undertaking community development.

Key takeaways

- Widely available, detailed, and consistent risk information can enable early identification of hazards and improve response coordination.
- Developing robust hazard information requires close coordination between ministries and scientific organizations involved in research and decision-making.
- Good communication between national and subnational governments, stakeholders, and local communities can help improve risk reduction practices and ensure a rapid relief response.

Sources: Bonasia R. and S. Lucatello. 2019. Linking Flood Susceptibility Mapping and Governance in Mexico for Flood Mitigation: A Participatory Approach Model. *Atmosphere*, 10(8); GFDRR. 2016. Country Profile: Mexico. Global Facility for Disaster Reduction and Recovery; OECD. 2013b. Reviews of Risk Management Policies: Mexico 2013. Paris: OECD Publishing; UNDP. 2014. Mexico: Country Case Study: How Law and Regulation Support Disaster Risk Reduction. New York: United Nations Development Programme. World Bank and GFDRR. 2012. Mexico Natural Disaster Fund—A Review. Washington, DC: International Bank for Reconstruction and Development/ World Bank.

It is possible to integrate fiscal sustainability assessments and climate-related risk information into a wide range of modeling approaches commonly leveraged by CFAs, including macrostructural models and revenue forecasting. CFAs usually use macrostructural models—general equilibrium models that assess the entire macroeconomy—for forecasting, economic policy, and budget planning. It is possible to integrate parameters to capture major climate impacts in these models. For example, the World Bank has expanded Pakistan's macrostructural model to include outcomes such as economic damage from heat and rainfall and map the connections between policy levers, fiscal aggregates, and climate outcomes (Burns, Jooste, and Schwerhoff 2021). The model introduces damage functions to capture how physical climate-related risks might affect economic activity (labor and agricultural productivity) and functions that represent how adaptation investments might mitigate climate damages to the economy, providing an evidence base for CFA policymakers on the impacts of climate change and policies on key macroeconomic variables (Burns, Jooste, and Schwerhoff 2021). The approach adopted by the World Bank has high technical requirements but demonstrates how to build climate-related risks into existing modeling frameworks.

CFAs can use tax revenue forecasts to assess potential changes in public resources. A common methodology uses GDP forecasts and calculates revenue changes based on assumptions (IMF 2020a). It is also possible to estimate the effect of asymmetrical shocks to the economy—such as a climate-related risk that predominantly affects the agriculture sector—by forecasting tax revenue at a sector, rather than aggregate, level (IMF 2020a). For example, Australia forecasts how changes in sector outlooks will impact business investment, allowing the CFA to, for example, determine that an expected decline in mining investment will lead to a real GDP growth detraction (IMF 2018).

Key Resources for Central Finance Agency Stakeholders

Climate Change and Long-Term Fiscal Sustainability (OECD 2021): Describing the long-term fiscal impacts from climate risks and adaptation, this paper provides guidance for governments on how to better assess the financial impacts of climate hazards and enhance fiscal risk evaluations and management to better respond to policies.

Macro-Fiscal Implications of Adaptation to Climate Change (Aligishiev, Massetti, and Bellon 2022): This report outlines the importance of conducting cost–benefit analyses to translate adaptation principles and estimates of climate impacts into effective policies. It provides information on useful methods and models for estimating the benefits, costs, and adaptation needs of residual risks from climate change.

Technical Guidance on Comprehensive Risk Assessment and Planning in the Context of Climate Change (UNDRR and GIZ 2022): This guidance provides recommendations on how to comprehensively assess, reduce and/or address risks through planning in the context of climate change. It is useful for understanding the main challenges in linking risk information to policy and offers good practice recommendations for integrating disaster risk management and climate change adaptation approaches.

3 Fiscal Risk Management and Strategies

The outcomes of a climate impact assessment can inform the approaches CFAs take to manage fiscal risks and promote a more resilient economy. Fiscal risks are potential deviations between actual and expected fiscal outcomes that affect CFAs' ability to finance planned expenditures and support national objectives. The risks can vary in probability, from small, regular occurrences to extreme events that are rare but highly affect fiscal health. CFAs may face a variety of climate-related fiscal risks, which they can identify and prioritize in fiscal sustainability assessments, as was described in Chapter 2.

The objective of fiscal risk management and strategy is to balance short-term funding needs and macroeconomic stability with long-term fiscal sustainability. An effective fiscal risk management strategy includes a set of CFA actions to reduce the likelihood or impact of unplanned shocks to government revenue streams, disruptions to the economy, or unsustainable debt (IMF 2020b). Fiscal management related to climate risks primarily focuses on managing acute risks. While chronic risks can have a significant impact on fiscal health, particularly in the long term, countries typically manage these through adaptation strategies. Chronic risk are less likely than acute risks to lead to fiscal volatility.

This chapter explores approaches and actions CFAs can take to manage risks based on data on climate-related risks. These include: actions to manage exposures by defining risk ownership and clarifying government liabilities; approaches to strategically manage fiscal risks by reducing, retaining, and transferring them; and methodologies for choosing cost-effective risk financing instruments.

CFAs can build up these approaches and actions at different levels to develop a robust fiscal risk management strategy. A good place to start is developing an understanding of the degree of intervention needed to manage fiscal risks and allocating funds. More advanced approaches involve using risk information to define the sources of risks and then taking action to limit these where possible, or to finance unmitigable risks. At the most advanced levels, CFAs can clearly define their sources of risk, identify where they allocate payments, and use risk financing instruments to meet those needs in a dynamic, cost-effective way.

Approaches to Risk Assignment

Assigning risks can provide clarity on the scale of a government's contingent liabilities. Risk assignment is the predefined allocation of who bears responsibility for risks. The objective is to clearly define risk ownership in a way that balances the costs of risk allocation, facilitates socioeconomic stability, and creates incentives for risk mitigation. By clarifying the scale of their direct risk exposures, CFAs can better leverage impact assessments to identify and quantify the impacts of climate-related risk on fiscal health. A more complete view of fiscal exposure can help CFAs assess whether they can take mitigating steps or need to manage risks through other approaches (IMF 2016).

Assigning risks can also create incentives for efficient risk management. In general, those with the power to take mitigating actions can also bear the risk most efficiently (IMF 2016). So, ensuring that these actors also have incentive to mitigate risks can help support efficient risk management. For example, if firms are responsible for bearing the costs of flooding, they have a higher incentive to invest in flood-resilient infrastructure or buy insurance. The South Africa case study (Box 3.1) demonstrates how the risk allocation structure within a PPP design can create incentives for risk mitigation, reducing contingent liabilities. But there are also circumstances where the private sector, households, or subnational governments cannot bear risks, due to excessive costs, inaccessible markets, or information barriers (IMF 2020b). It is therefore important to consider both incentives and capacity when assigning risks (IMF 2016).

Box 3.1: Allocating Risk: Lessons from South Africa

South Africa has begun expanding investment in renewable energy projects through public–private partnerships (PPPs). As of 2022, the government had more than 114 active PPP projects and more than $27.2 billion in investment, with renewable energy PPPs making up 7 of the 10 largest projects. A significant risk to these projects is that renewable energy can be vulnerable to physical climate change. For example, extreme heat can damage transmission infrastructure, reduce solar power efficiency, and require maintenance shutdowns or investment in new infrastructure. Although this has not happened in South African PPPs, it represents a large source of fiscal risk exposure.

South Africa relies on several types of analysis to understand risk exposure and inform project selection decisions. First, the government conducts a cost–benefit analysis to identify and quantify financial flows of projects and the potential impacts of crucial risks. For example, it can examine how acute climate events might hinder operations and consequently reduce the partnership's financial viability. Next, it quantifies its contingent liabilities by running best- and worst-case scenario analysis to determine the potential costs of various events that could make the liabilities materialize. However, there may be events, such as coronavirus disease (COVID-19), that cause contingent liabilities to materialize but are not included in scenario analysis. These scenarios are not stipulated in the contracts and may cause a downward bias in the government's estimation of risk-related costs.

Continued monitoring of contingent liabilities enables South Africa to adjust to new climate and fiscal risk information. South Africa's Assets and Liability Management Division is a central oversight body tasked with assessing risk-mitigating strategies of PPPs, state-owned enterprises, and local governments. In tandem with a specialized PPP unit, this body oversees project liability risks and requires quarterly financial statements and performance reports. Noncompliant partnerships get technical assistance for project design, implementation, and monitoring.

South Africa's PPP management framework is designed to limit the scale of the government's contingent liabilities and incentivize community investment. The country's Renewable Energy Independent Power Producer Procurement Programme reduces government liabilities by explicitly defining rules around sovereign support, ensuring partners have enough funds to avoid government intervention. The government also encourages competition between bidders to facilitate private investments in local communities by including weights on their contributions to local economic development as well as price objectives in bid evaluations. Central finance agencies could use a similar approach to incentivize bidders to reduce climate-related risks, by including criteria in bid evaluations.

Key takeaways

- Central finance agencies can use cost–benefit and scenario analyses to quantitatively assess contingent liabilities and make risk-informed partnership decisions.
- Robust monitoring and evaluation systems can help governments dynamically assess changing climate-related risks.
- Partnership frameworks can explicitly limit the scope of government liabilities and build incentive structures that support socioeconomic outcomes and reduce partnership risks.

Sources: Irwin, T. and T. Mokdad. 2010. *Managing Contingent Liabilities in Public–Private Partnerships*; Naude R. and A. Eberhard. 2017. *The South African Renewable Energy IPP Procurement Programme: Review Lessons Learned and Proposals to Reduce Transaction Costs*; PPPLRC. n.d. *Countries: South Africa*. https://pppknowledgelab.org/countries/south-africa; World Bank. Benchmarking Infrastructure Development, Global Data: PPP. https://bpp.worldbank.org/global?survey=PPP; World Bank. 2017. *Establishing a Fiscal Risk Management Department in the Ministry of Finance of Serbia*. Washington, DC.

The appropriate approach and actions for managing these risks depend on the nature of the risks, the institutional environment, and the costs and benefits of risk allocation within the economy. CFAs can use risk assignment actions to manage risks associated with public partnerships and the private sector.

Public partnership risk can arise when PPPs, SOEs, or subnational government operations are set up so the government is primarily liable for the impacts of climate-related risks on operations. For example, after Hurricane Joaquin hit the Bahamas in 2015, the government paid a portion of its $30 million budget for power infrastructure to Bahamas Power and Light to replace power infrastructure damaged in the storm (IDB 2017). This kind of spending shrinks government accounts and can increase expenditure needed to cover guaranteed debt obligations (IMF 2016).

Private sector risk arises when businesses and enterprises fail to manage risks effectively. The government may incur additional expenditures if it is assumed to be responsible for supporting businesses significantly affected by climate-related risks. This can also affect macroeconomic performance and linked fiscal outcomes such as tax revenues and foreign exchange reserves (IMF 2016).

CFAs can develop policies that directly limit explicit liabilities, creating incentives for partners to limit risky behavior. These include regulatory tools, financial instrument arrangements, and fiscal policy rules to clarify that partners must carry the financial burden in the event of a downturn or shock. A few examples illustrate fiscal policy actions that CFAs can use to deal with climate-related risks.

- **Limiting explicit liabilities based on financial performance and climate-related risk exposure:** CFAs can link government payouts to SOEs, PPPs, and subnational government financial performance or risk-reducing activities (IMF 2016). Doing so can either directly reduce explicit liabilities or provide incentives for partners to mitigate their own climate-related risks, which reduces explicit or implicit liabilities. Imposing these criteria can come at a cost if they require oversight and mechanisms to enforce compliance. In Chile, for example, a finance ministry approval process for PPP contracts allows the CFA to evaluate possible government contingent liabilities and adapt contracts accordingly. Since 1991, only three of 59 projects have activated the minimum revenue guarantee (World Bank 2017). The Chilean process does not include climate-related risks but has the framework and capacity to do so. Similar evaluations that include information about climate-related risk can limit fiscal exposure as climate-related risks become more relevant.

- **Caps on government-backed insurance schemes:** CFAs can limit liabilities by reducing the scale of insurance schemes (IMF 2016). Governments may consider whether alternative insurance mechanisms are available on the market. For example, the US government's Federal Emergency Management Agency's nationwide flood insurance program limits payouts for building property at $250,000 to ensure adequate coverage for property owners, while maintaining the potential strain on fiscal health (Congressional Research Service 2021). However, these schemes are typically offered to vulnerable populations or in areas where risk is concentrated and cannot be mitigated, potentially making private insurance prohibitively expensive. Removing insurance schemes with no viable alternatives might add to fiscal risk by exacerbating vulnerable populations' financial exposure to systemic risks. Another option is to introduce deductibles to reduce overhead costs and align incentives, while protecting vulnerable populations from untenable risks.

- **Linking government loans to climate-related risk and risk mitigation:** CFAs can develop policies that limit loan size to other sovereigns, subnational governments, PPPs, or SOEs based on reserves or overall exposure to climate risks. This can encourage firms to invest in risk mitigation strategies in exchange for better loan conditions (IMF 2016). For example, in Brazil, Japan, the Republic of Korea, and Spain, CFAs impose restrictions loans based on subnational governments' ability to service debt in the event of a materialized contingent liability (Singh and Plekhanov 2005). Such a policy can reduce the required financial assistance resulting from climate-related and default risks. However, small firms may have limited capacity to invest in risk reduction, and imposing caps on loans can stifle economic growth (IMF 2016).

- **Mandatory limits on debt stock or minimum tax requirements for subnational governments:** CFAs can regulate subnational economies to reduce the likelihood that government bailouts will be necessary (IMF 2016). For example, in Romania, local government borrowing is capped at 30% of average revenue in the previous 3 years. To ensure compliance, local governments publish revenue, expenditures, and debt monthly, with financial penalties when the limits are exceeded (World Bank 2017). An important consideration in the design of fiscal rules is whether subnational governments can comply or have the resources to absorb penalties for noncompliance (IMF 2016). And while the expectation of bailouts can lead subnational governments to take excessive risks, failing to provide financial support might have political ramifications.

- **Collaborating with humanitarian-focused third parties:** CFAs may want to assume risk ownership to protect vulnerable households. Defining risk ownership between the government and social insurance programs can protect vulnerable populations and lessen implicit government liabilities (IMF 2020b). CFAs may therefore consider collaborating with humanitarian-focused third parties to meet humanitarian needs while limiting government expenditures. For example, Kenya's Hunger and Safety Net Programme is a government-led initiative partially financed through the World Bank that provides cash transfers to farming communities in the event of a drought (HSNP n.d.). This program makes implicit liabilities explicit, while providing humanitarian protection.

CFAs can also create rules or incentives that support businesses and households to manage climate-related risks. These policies can include market-based incentives, regulation, and information dissemination through the following actions:

- **Mandating insurance coverage for systemic risks:** While it is not possible to reduce all risks, CFAs that mandate insurance coverage for specific types of risk can lower implicit government liabilities. But it is important to consider whether the targeted population can afford mandated insurance. In some cases, governments might need to subsidize the insurance product to ensure compliance. For example, Türkiye's Catastrophe Insurance Pool mandates earthquake[4] coverage within urban areas to reduce government liabilities but offers subsidies to facilitate compliance (IMF 2020b). CFAs can also encourage uptake by requiring insurance companies to pool risks. For example, UK insurance companies have to contribute to a flood risk reinsurance fund, which reimburses insurers for flood damage claims and enables them to reduce the cost of insurance in flood-prone areas (Browning 2023). This approach allows the CFA to assign risks and more accurately assess expenditures in the event of a climate shock.

- **Imposing capital requirements for financial institutions:** CFAs can require lenders and insurers to hold enough funds to cover losses from an acute climate event. For example, the Bank of England declared that banks and insurers in the UK must meet additional capital requirements for assets carrying climate risks (Makortoff 2021). Financial institutions can prepare for losses and discourage risk aggregation by considering budgetary needs in high-risk scenarios. This helps protect vulnerable sectors and geographies and can reduce the need for government bailouts. However, if banks and insurers reduce their lending and coverage to meet requirements, this could impede economic growth. Advance notice and incremental rollout could give insurers and lenders enough time to obtain adequate funds and reduce economic impacts (Mosk 2018).

- **Specifying recovery spending strategies:** CFAs can outline recovery spending strategies for different probabilistic scenarios to dissuade the private sector from relying on bailouts to prevent corporate failure. Specifying risks aims to make the scope of the government's liabilities explicit, make risk assignment credible, and encourage private corporations to mitigate risks. For example, private entities in Colombia are not eligible for government guarantees to encourage self-sufficient risk management (Bachmair 2016). However, some firms may recognize their importance for the local or national economy and count on support by regarding themselves as "too big to fail". (IMF 2016).

- **Using market instruments to incentivize behaviors:** CFAs can use market-based incentives to limit risky behavior and lower the concentration of activities in high-risk areas (IMF 2016). For example, to reduce the fiscal impacts of flooding, the Government of the People's Republic of China introduced a farmer relocation subsidy that offers financial assistance for farmers to move away from floodplains (Wang et al. 2020). CFAs can use indirect increases in market prices to discourage further investment in high-risk areas and mitigate household and business exposure to climate-related risks, thus reducing their explicit or assumed risks government liabilities. However, imposing a tax during a period of economic stress may not be politically salient, and introducing new taxes, especially in post-disaster environments, may require robust institutional infrastructure and could cost more than the revenue generated or the risks reduced (IMF 2016).

---

4   Although earthquakes are not a climate-related risk, this example demonstrates that countries can apply insurance policies to climate-related risks.

Approaches to Managing Fiscal Risk Exposure

A fiscal risk management strategy can help CFAs to manage exposure to climate-related risks cost-effectively and facilitate long-term economic development. Fiscal risk exposure represents the magnitude of fiscal resources that could be at risk. As discussed in Chapter 2, unmitigated exposure to climate-related risks can lead to reduced government services, increased borrowing, and macroeconomic volatility (IMF 2016). Effective management of fiscal risk exposure involves developing an approach with an appropriate balance between:

- **Risk reduction actions**, which lower governments' liabilities by directly reducing the size of a risk. For climate-related risk, this is typically through adaptation investment in infrastructure or policy to limit implicit risks.[5]

- **Risk retention actions**, which are fiscal buffers—such as budget reallocations or contingency funds—can help the government manage the costs of climate-related liabilities. These actions tend to be appropriate for smaller risks, where government has the resources to fund contingent liabilities (Global Disaster Preparedness Center 2013).

- **Risk transfer actions**, which pass loss and damage risks from one party on to another, as done by an insurance contract. These actions tend to have a premium and be expensive to hold, so risk transfer is typically most appropriate for low-probability and high-cost risks.

Although there is no singular approach to balancing these actions, to develop a fit-for-purpose approach, CFAs can consider three main criteria: the evidence base, cost-effectiveness, and adaptability. Does the strategy address fiscal sustainability priorities as identified in climate impact assessments? Are the actions deployed cost-effectively? And is the strategy flexible to new and evolving information about climate-related risk?

CFAs can develop measurable fiscal health indicators to inform risk management needs. Approaches to managing risks often involve trade-offs. For example, increases in risk transfer actions may reduce macroeconomic volatility but will come at a higher opportunity cost. How CFAs align their priorities with these tradeoffs will depend on fiscal health and the type, size, and frequency of the climate-related risks they face. Typically, these will align with fiscal health indicators chosen by the government. Barbados, for example, has a debt to GDP ratio of 138%. To minimize further impacts from climate-related risks, the government has expanded its management capacity by securing a $80 million contingent loan to protect public finances (IDB 2020). Setting clear fiscal health indicators and priorities can help guide decisions. An increasing number of modeling tools are available that help link climate-related financing needs, indicators of fiscal health, and risk management tools. For example, the International Institute for Applied Systems Analysis's CATSIM model identifies financing gaps based on fiscal inputs and climate-related risks, finds appropriate objectives, and selects the risk management tools to meet those objectives (IIASA 2020).

A risk layering approach can help CFAs develop a cost-effective risk management strategy. Risk layering is an approach for combining financing instruments to cover risks of varying sizes and frequencies when economically viable risk reduction measures are unavailable. The principle of risk layering is to use low-cost financing mechanisms to cover low-cost risks, and then layer more expensive instruments to cover infrequent and very severe risks (Meenan Ward, and Muir-Wood 2019). Risk layering can be a cost-effective way to manage risks. This can be important for countries that are credit-constrained and unable to finance large costs. The case study from the Philippines (Box 3.2) shows this approach in practice. Using well-designed risk transfer instruments can deliver efficient emergency relief and recovery, further reducing fiscal impacts.

---

[5]   Risk reduction through adaptation financing and investment is discussed in Chapter 4.

Box 3.2: Layering Risk: Lessons from the Philippines

Typhoons are a significant source of fiscal and socioeconomic risk in the Philippines. Average annual economic damage from typhoons and earthquakes in the country is estimated at more than $3.5 billion. In 2013, Typhoon Haiyan caused around $13 billion in damages, with the private sector bearing nearly 80% of the costs. Nearly three-quarters of the population remains exposed to a combination of hazards, posing a significant humanitarian and fiscal risk.

In response, the Philippines has developed a robust risk financing framework to build fiscal sustainability. The framework uses the three tiers of risk finance: local retention, national retention, and risk transfer through international insurance and capital markets. The local risk retention for smaller risks develops a manageable level of risk ownership and reduces national government liabilities. National risk retention and international capital markets contain fiscal costs for larger risks.

To address lower-severity risks, the Philippines established national management funds to finance post-disaster relief and recovery. Congress allocates funds toward the National Disaster Risk Reduction Management Fund, while the Local Disaster Risk Reduction and Calamity Fund requires local governments to set aside at least 5% of their annual budget toward disaster financing, with any unspent resources accruing in the fund for up to 5 years. On top of these allocations, the government has set up a line of contingent finance with the World Bank for an additional $500 million on declaring a national emergency. These funds enable the government to use budget allocations to absorb average annual losses while using higher-cost mechanisms, such as contingency credit and budget reallocation, for larger climate-related risks.

The government manages more severe climate risks with mechanisms that transfer risk to insurers. In 2019, the Philippines purchased $225 million in earthquake and tropical cyclone coverage in form of insurance-linked security from the World Bank. The risk transfer is linked to the severity of the catastrophe and dependent on a modeled trigger. This easily measured parameter can be used as a proxy for expected losses. For example, the typhoon trigger depends on wind speed, which is easily measured and highly correlated with losses. The insurance was triggered for Super Typhoon Rai (known locally as Odette) in 2021 but not for Tropical Storm Megi, which is estimated to have caused $91 million in damages.

The government is seeking to expand its risk transfer mechanisms to address funding gaps. Its current approach covers medium-severity climate-related risks but will not adequately finance high-cost events like Typhoon Haiyan in 2013. As a result, a high-severity event is likely to require external intervention. The Department of Finance is looking for additional mechanisms to address high-severity risks, as the bulk of financing for such risks goes toward relief and recovery, with limited resources for reconstruction.

Key takeaways

- Building local risk ownership can reduce the national government's contingent liabilities and ensure funding is effectively distributed at the community level.
- Budget allocation is an efficient first source of financing for climate shocks, while risk transfer instruments provide coverage for low-frequency, high-severity events.
- Central finance agencies seeking similar debt instruments can engage with development agencies that can help facilitate coverage for high-severity climate shocks—for example, the World Bank offers Catastrophe Deferred Drawdown Options to International Bank for Reconstruction and Development–eligible borrowers, provided they have some form of disaster risk management program with the appropriate macroeconomic policy framework that ensures funds reach intended beneficiaries.

Sources: Artemis. The Artemis Catastrophe Bond and Insurance-Linked Securities Deal Directory. https://www.artemis.bm/deal-directory/ibrd-car-123-124/; Global Disaster Preparedness Center. 2013. Local Disaster Risk Reduction and Management Fund. GFDRR. 2014. Recovery and Reconstruction Planning the Aftermath of Typhoon Haiyan. Global Facility for Disaster Reduction and Recovery. https://www.gfdrr.org/en/publication/recovery-and-reconstruction-planning-aftermath-typhoon-haiyan; OECD. 2022. *Building Financial Resilience to Climate Impacts. A Framework for Governments to Manage the Risks of Losses and Damages.* Paris: OECD Publishing; Philippine Institute for Development Studies. 2017. *A Review of Philippine Government Disaster Financing for Recovery and Reconstruction;* Signer, B. and R. Poulter. 2021. *Disaster Risk Insurance: 5 Insights from the Philippines.* https://blogs.worldbank.org/climatechange/disaster-risk-insurance-5-insights-philippines.

As climate-related risks evolve and increase, dynamic approaches to risk management can help build fiscal sustainability. Such an approach builds flexibility, allowing CFAs to adjust their strategy to new climate-related risk information without incurring significant costs. Risk layering helps minimize the costs of the management strategy. Building a dynamic risk management portfolio can similarly help minimize costs over a long time horizon. The following examples highlight actions and approaches CFAs can take to dynamically adapt to new data:

- **Establishing a central oversight body:** South Africa's National Disaster Management Centre models different regions' risks and vulnerabilities by accounting for hazards, institutional resilience capabilities, and wider political and socioeconomic vulnerabilities. It collects and assesses data annually, to report on disaster expenditure in line with funding frameworks determined in the PFM cycle. This framework continuously monitors new risks, enabling the agency to accurately assess the costs and impacts of disasters and adjust its risk management strategy and funding accordingly (OECD 2015).

- **Using adaptable instruments:** Following a wave of climate-related disasters, Barbados, with IMF support, restructured its bonds to include a clause that provides loan extensions in the event of a hurricane (Waithe 2019). This instrument is flexible to new climate-related risk information and allows the CFA to update its financing strategy in response. As a result, Barbados can issue new bonds without the danger of incurring unsustainable debt.

- **Building back better:** Mexico's Natural Disasters Fund (FONDEN) regularly assesses disaster impacts, enabling the government to update its recovery and reconstruction spending, prioritize financing toward post-disaster needs based on new information, and reduce its exposure to anticipated climate-related risks (World Bank 2017).

- **Adopting climate-responsive PFM:** CFAs regularly monitor and adjust the PFM cycle, making it an inherently dynamic approach (Gonguet et al. 2021). As climate-related risks become more material, CFAs can consider linking this information into budget oversight to improve ownership of risks. For example, the Public Expenditure and Financial Accountability program provides a framework that informs CFAs how regulations, institutions, systems, procedures, and processes contribute to climate change and government vulnerability to physical risks throughout the budget cycle (PEFA n.d.).

Approaches to Instrument Selection

CFAs can implement risk management actions with a structured, evidence-based approach to instrument selection. When deployed appropriately, risk financing instruments—the mechanisms that retain or transfer the financial costs of climate-related risks to reduce their fiscal impact—can be cost-effective for meeting climate-related risk management goals. But instruments vary in design and effectiveness for managing different types of climate-related risk and meeting objectives (OECD 2015). For example, drought risks may require instruments that are quick to disburse to meet urgent humanitarian needs, while flood risks may require longer-term reconstruction financing. So, it is important to select them with care.

Four main steps are involved in selecting appropriate instruments and assessing their ongoing performance in meeting risk management needs:

1. **Determining success criteria:** What are the priorities in instrument selection?
2. **Identifying and appraising options:** What instruments are available? How well do they perform against success criteria?
3. **Procurement:** What do CFAs need to do to obtain the selected instrument?
4. **Monitoring and evaluation:** What can CFAs do to ensure the instrument acts as intended?

Risk financing instruments can address multiple forms of risk exposure and risk-related financing challenges. Hence, selecting an appropriate instrument requires careful consideration when prioritizing aspects of risk. Issues to consider include: the source of the fiscal risk exposure (e.g., contingent liabilities and reduced tax revenue), the size of exposure, the likelihood of risk, financing needs, and the costs if financing fails to reach the intended recipients. When selecting these instruments, CFAs can consider five design features:

- **Speed:** How quickly can it disburse funding?

- **Cost:** How affordable is it? Are there more cost-effective alternatives?

- **Coverage:** How much financial protection does it offer? If payout is determined by a trigger, what is it, and how likely is it to be reached in the event of a climate disaster?

- **Flexibility:** Does the financing instrument provide funding for multiple types of climate-related risks? Is it possible for the funds to be diverted for other uses?

- **Reliability:** How reliable are the selected instruments? Are there any other barriers that will prevent funding from getting to its intended target?

Prioritizing the most important features for managing specific fiscal risks can also help CFAs shortlist appropriate instruments. Examples of instrument selection approaches to address specific risk management challenges include:

- **Providing humanitarian flood relief for vulnerable groups:** Several pilot programs in Bangladesh demonstrate the value of speed through their use of forecast-based-financing, a form of index insurance, to provide vulnerable households with funds before flooding occurs (IFRC 2021). As well as helping households meet immediate needs, this rapid disbursal approach can be cost-effective, lowering the cost of emergency response by as much as 50% (Climate Centre 2016).

- **Managing local government relief costs:** In Viet Nam, states are required to contribute 2%–5% of their budget to a fund reserved for paying out explicit and implicit liabilities after a physical hazard (OECD 2015). If the fund does not cover needs, the government can tap into a national reserve fund that is adjusted every year to account for new data on climate-related risk and cover expected annual climate-disaster costs (OECD 2015). Budget allocations and reallocations can offer a flexible, reliable source of financing for frequent and smaller risks, enabling CFAs to cover contingent liabilities without increasing debt.

- **Financing infrastructure repairs:** In Australia, subnational governments are primarily responsible for post-disaster financing. For example, to ensure adequate funding, the Queensland Treasury established the Queensland Government Insurance Fund, a mandated self-insurance scheme for state government agencies and bodies. This Treasury-run fund identifies risk exposure and covers liabilities for any loss or damage to state assets, ensuring substantial coverage for local governments (Waithe 2019). The program offers a breadth of reliable property catastrophe coverage from various risks while ensuring subnational governments are responsible for their own risks.

Outcomes will depend on instrument design and the local context. CFAs can review instruments against success criteria to identify the most suitable instruments for their local context. As well as mapping different risk financing instruments onto financing criteria (Figure 3.1), their engagement with donors, international agencies, insurers, and insurance brokers can help CFAs determine instrument suitability, viability, and affordability for a given climate-related risk financing challenge. For example, in 2019, the UN Central Emergency Response Fund allocated about $10 million to Malawi for the government to develop a risk-financing strategy against agriculture losses. To facilitate a rapid response, the government piloted forecast-based financing system for floods and droughts that would allocate anticipatory funds to the insured. However, the costs of the trigger's inaccuracy outweighed the benefits of rapid deployment, and the project shifted focus away from floods to drought, which had a more reliable trigger (Getliffe 2022).

Figure 3.1: Disaster Risk Financing Taxonomy

		Risk holder: What is the capacity and need of the risk holder?				Purpose: What will funds be spent on?			Timing: When is funding needed?			Risk level: What level of risk is being addressed? (return period)		
Action	**Instrument**	Individual	Community	Municipality	Sovereign	Life and livelihood	Operational	Physical assets	Preparation	Response	Recovery	Annual	1–10 years	10–50+ years	50+ years
Risk retention	Budget retention			•	•		•			•		•	•		
Risk retention	Reserve funds	•	•	•	•	•	•	•		•	•	•	•		
Risk retention	Contingent loans				•		•			•	•		•	•	
Risk transfer	Micro-insurance	•	•			•		•		•	•		•	•	•
Risk transfer	Agriculture insurance	•	•			•				•	•		•	•	•
Risk transfer	Takaful and mutual insurance	•	•	•	•	•	•	•		•	•		•	•	•
Risk transfer	Insurance and reinsurance	•	•	•	•	•	•	•		•	•		•	•	•
Risk transfer	Catastrophe bonds			•	•	•	•	•		•	•			•	•
Risk transfer	Risk pools			•	•		•	•		•	•		•	•	•

Source: Meenan, C., J. Ward, and R. Muir-Wood. 2019. *Disaster Risk Finance: A Toolkit*. Bonn: GIZ.

Once CFAs have selected the potential instruments, they can use scenario analysis to test outcomes against priorities and fiscal health indicators. First, they define impact channels and stakeholders of interest. For example, assessing a drought risk financing portfolio could help develop a set of assumptions around mitigating impacts on agricultural losses, food imports, and humanitarian assistance costs. Next, they can model the impacts of instruments using appraisal tools consistent with those used in public policy appraisal. For example, the UK Government issued The Green Book, which offers guidance on how to appraise policies, programs, and projects, such as risk financing, by assessing the costs, benefits, and risks of alternative ways to meet government objectives (HM Treasury 2022). Building the expected impacts of the instruments into qualitative or quantitative assessments can provide a view on how well the instruments perform against multiple macroeconomic indicators and fiscal sustainability priorities. CFAs can use this multicriteria analysis to compare the costs and potential benefits of different combinations of instruments, assessing outcomes to select the combination that best fits their needs (Meenan, Ward, and Muir-Wood 2019).

CFAs can assess the feasibility of portfolios by sounding out markets and earmarking necessary funding. To determine the viability and cost-effectiveness of selected instruments, CFAs can contact the entities offering them to gauge market interest and options for cost, coverage, and structure. Once deemed viable, CFAs can amend their budget to earmark funding, using supportive legislation within the PFM budget formulation and approval to codify funding sources if needed (OECD 2015). They can then use this funding to buy or develop the desired risk financing instrument. Purchasing risk transfer mechanisms can require further engagement with donors, insurers, or brokers to develop an appropriate arrangement. CFAs might need to build institutional capacity within ministries or subnational governments to ensure funding reaches its intended beneficiaries.

CFAs can adapt to evolving climate-related risks by establishing a central oversight body to monitor, evaluate, and refine risk financing portfolios. The evolving character of climate-related risks means that CFAs need to have dynamic policies and strategies. An IMF report on fiscal risk management good practices suggests establishing a dedicated unit tasked with assessing whether risk mitigation is a good-practice approach to monitoring the effectiveness of risk financing instruments. Such a unit can oversee risks, assess risk instruments, and make recommendations for improvement (IMF 2016). For example, Peru established the Risk Management Division (DGR) to oversee fiscal risks, determine where improvements can be made, and make recommendations for the CFA to consider in making risk management decisions (World Bank and GFDRR 2015). To date, the DGR, with the Ministry of Finance, has conducted substantive evidence-based risk assessments, streamlined disaster funding sources in the PFM cycle, established guidelines for use of funds, and bolstered its disaster risk management strategy by using multiple instruments (World Bank and GFDRR 2016).

Key Resources for Central Finance Agency Stakeholders

Analyzing and Managing Fiscal Risks: Best Practices (IMF 2016): This best practice report on the implications of fiscal risks and how they can be managed provides an overview of fiscal risk analysis, fiscal risk management, and the costs and benefits of different fiscal risk management approaches.

Disaster Risk Financing: A Global Survey of Practices and Challenges (OECD 2015): This paper explores a wide range of approaches to disaster risk financing and its consequences for economic development, with case studies of practiced risk financing approaches.

Disaster Risk Finance: A Toolkit (Meenan, Ward, and Muir-Wood 2019): This toolkit provides practical guidance on how to use different risk financing instruments and for which circumstance. It is structured as a series of steps to help decision-makers understand, reduce, and finance risks.

Dull Disasters? How Planning Ahead Will Make a Difference (Clarke and Dercon 2016): Exploring a range of risk financing solutions that have been implemented to respond to dull disasters, this book provides an overview of effective and ineffective approaches, using historical case studies to guide future practice.

Fiscal Policy: How to Manage the Fiscal Costs of Natural Disasters (IMF 2018): This book provides guidance on how to design, implement, and use fiscal buffers to protect fiscal sustainability from disasters triggered by natural hazards.

Investment in Disaster Risk Management in Europe Makes Economic Sense (World Bank 2021): This report provides an overview of the economic benefits of investing in disaster and preparedness to climate-related risks.

Managing Fiscal Risks Under Stress (IMF 2020): This note discusses strategies and steps governments can take to deal with fiscal risks while under budgetary pressure, focusing on the macro fiscal and budgetary risk caused by COVID-19 and how governments can strengthen overall public financial management capacities to dampen these risks.

4 Evidence-Informed Adaptation Financing and Investment

The costs of coping with climate-related risks and impacts are increasing. Between 2017 and 2019, adaptation investment amounted to just 4%–8% of total climate finance globally. The Intergovernmental Panel on Climate Change estimates that, as climate-related risks increase, adaptation investment needs in developing countries will reach nearly $300 billion a year by 2050 (WRI 2022). The costs of meeting these needs could be as much as 10% of GDP, particularly in climate-vulnerable island states, putting more pressure on often already-strained public finances (Aligishiev, Massetti, and Bellon 2022).

Well-designed and efficiently implemented adaptation investments can reduce climate-related impacts while delivering socioeconomic benefits. Estimates of cost–benefit ratios for adaptation projects range from 2:1 to 10:1 (GCA 2019). Investing in adaptation can similarly reduce fiscal risks and build economic resilience (Dabla-Norris et al. 2021; Pigato 2019). The largest annual adaptation finance gaps in developing countries are in infrastructure, energy, costal protection, and other built environment sectors, amounting to up to $50 billion annually to 2050 (Tall et al. 2021).

This chapter explores approaches and actions CFAs can take to efficiently mobilize resources at scale, using climate-related risk information as an evidence base for making decisions. CFAs play vital roles in mobilizing both public and private adaptation finance and investment. They can also help coordinate these actions to ensure a collectively sufficient response. This is particularly important for adaptation investments, which may be underprovided, if left to the private sector alone (Pigato 2019).

To ensure public adaptation investment and financing is efficient, CFAs can mobilize public funds for adaptation and ensure that investments are evidence-based, cost-effective, and align with national priorities (Coalition of Finance Ministers for Climate Action 2022). This involves decisions on both how investors spend public resources and which fiscal tools they use.

CFAs can also help mobilize adaptation finance from private investment, international public finance, and green bonds (Coalition of Finance Ministers for Climate Action 2022). To attract and scale up private finance, CFAs can help remove barriers to investment and develop strategies to leverage the private sector's increasing focus on investing in sustainability (Eguino, Delgado, and Lopes 2021). They can also support finance sector development, which may be particularly important in countries with underdeveloped markets.

CFAs should consider three dimensions in their approach to adaptation investment and financing: the evidence base and prioritization framework, financing strategy, and governance and mainstreaming.[6] They can consider how evidence-driven tools and instruments can be used to identify investment priorities, whether the adaptation financing strategy supports cost-effective adaptation investments, and whether their fiscal policy leverages governance frameworks for resource allocation and existing PFM processes.

---

[6] These dimensions were identified based on a review of literature on the role of climate risk information for adaptation financing and investment.

Approaches to Mobilizing Efficient Public Adaptation Investment Fund Financing

The public sector is a vital source of adaptation finance and investment. Public investment can be an important source of finance for meeting substantial adaptation capital requirements, particularly in developing countries, where adaptation is often more necessary than mitigation and international sources may be insufficient (Allan et al. 2019; Amirali 2020). Adapting to climate-related risks requires large-scale investment in public goods, such as resilient infrastructure, which the private sector might be unwilling to provide (Bellon and Massetti 2022a). This creates a crucial role for the public sector to act on climate-related risk adaptation. As adaptation needs are significant and expected to increase, public spending needs to be managed carefully to align with adaptation priorities while meeting fiscal sustainability needs (Bellon and Massetti 2022b).

CFAs can mobilize efficient adaptation financing by increasing available resources for adaptation through innovative financing approaches, allocating budgets, and prioritizing investments. Climate-related risk information can help highlight the scale of adaptation finance needs, underscore how much funding is needed to respond to evolving risks, and assess the impact of expenditure on climate-related risk vulnerability (Oxford Policy Management 2021; GCA 2019).

Various examples are available showing how programmatic public adaptation initiatives can generate revenue and allocate budgets to adaptation activities. These include the Peoples' Survival Fund, a climate fund linked to national adaptation strategies in the Philippines and financed domestically (Box 4.1), and an innovative climate finance approach in Indonesia (Box 4.2). An example of another approach is hypothecated taxes or debt-for-adaptation swaps (GCA 2019). These include the United Nations Economic Commission for Latin America and the Caribbean's initiative that enables small island and low-lying coastal developing states in the Caribbean to obtain debt relief while increasing investment in adaptation and resilience (ECLAC n.d.).

Box 4.1: Domestic Climate Funds: Lessons from the Philippines

In 2012, the Philippines established a national adaptation fund in response to its high exposure to climate-related risks. The country is exposed to several climate-related risks, including typhoons, flooding, sea level rise, and tsunamis. The People's Survival Fund (PSF) was established in 2012 under the National Treasury to provide funding for adaptation and resilience projects. Funded by the national budget, it receives a minimum of ₱1 billion ($20 million)[a] each year, which can be supplemented by local government and private sector funding.

The PSF funds activities that target local adaptation efforts and are aligned with national and local climate-related risks and disaster risk reduction plans. It aims to cover financing gaps for projects that are aligned with national or local strategies, plans, and frameworks for climate-related risk adaptation and disaster risk reduction. It has three criteria for project prioritization: local poverty incidence, exposure to climate-related risk, and the existence of important biodiversity areas. The PSF covers a range of climate-exposed sectors, including water resource and land management, agriculture, and fisheries. Funded projects to date include a climate field school for farmers and fisherfolk, community-based ecological farming to build climate resilience, and disaster risk reduction projects.

The PSF uses climate-related risk information to identify vulnerabilities and supports information-sharing and early warning system activities. Its criteria indicate that project objectives should directly address climate-related risks identified by scientific and historical data on climate vulnerabilities. It also provides funding for establishing information networks and forecasting and early warning systems to improve planning and preparedness in response to climate-related risks. Support for such activities can help increase the use of risk information for adaptation by facilitating access to information and disseminating it.

Low project approval rates, due to stringent requirements, is a significant challenge for the PSF. Between 2012 and 2020, the fund received more than 170 project proposals, but approved only 6. Technical challenges in meeting strict criteria for vulnerability and effectiveness assessments pose a significant barrier to project approval. To address this and

continued on next page

Box 4.1 *continued*

unlock more funding for adaptation, the PSF has simplified its application criteria, reducing the original 14 requirements to four. Improving information on funding requirements for local governments could further facilitate access to PSF funding, enabling more targeted and successful applications.

Key takeaways

- Central finance agencies can use information on climate-related risk in their investment decisions by aligning project criteria with nationally identified priorities.
- Socioeconomic project criteria can also help ensure that climate and development priorities are aligned.
- It is important to strike a balance between rigorous evaluation criteria and ensuring applications are feasible and accessible.

[a] Based on the average 2021 exchange rate from the World Bank.
Sources: Department of Finance. 2020. *People's Survival Fund Seeks to Find Solution to Climate Crisis.* https://www.dof.gov.ph/peoples-survival-fund-seeks-to-find-solution-to-climate-crisis/; GGGI. 2022. *Support to the Operationalization of the People's Survival Fund.* Global Green Growth Institute. https://gggi.org/project/support-to-the-operationalization-of-the-peoples-survival-fund/; NICCDIES. 2022. *People's Survival Fund.* National Integrated Climate Change Database Information and Exchange System. https://niccdies.climate.gov.ph/climate-finance/people-survival-fund; OECD. 2020. *Common Ground Between the Paris Agreement and the Sendai Framework: Climate Change Adaptation and Disaster Risk Reduction.* Paris: OECD Publishing.

Box 4.2: Innovative Climate Finance: Lessons from Indonesia

Indonesia's climate change funding is predominantly domestic and dominated by public sources. The government provides 66% of climate change finance, while 34% comes from international public funds, the involvement of the private sector is considered quite limited due to inadequate financial incentives, regulatory framework constraints, and capacity deficiencies to address climate change challenges. From 2016 to 2020, the government spent an average of Rp84.9 trillion (or 4.1% of the annual state budget) on climate change-related activities, 22.1% on adaptation investments, and 77.9% on mitigation projects.

The Ministry of Finance encourages implementation of innovative public finance to enhance fiscal capacity and finance climate adaptation, through green bonds/sukuk (Sharia-compliant bonds), the Indonesia Environment Fund (BPDLH), the Adaptation Fund, the Global Environment Facility, Green Climate Fund, SDG Indonesia One (SIO), and the Indonesia Climate Change Trust Fund (ICCTF). However, most projects and activities are dominated by mitigation. In addition to green bonds, the government has successfully issued several green sukuk, starting in 2018. Based on the Sukuk Framework, climate adaptation (including disaster) is one of the eligible green projects—i.e., research leading to technology innovation with sustainability benefits, food security, flood mitigation, drought management, and public health management. In principle, the green sukuk uses the results of its climate budget tagging mechanism and channels investment toward and across green sectors with the most climate change impact.

In Indonesia, general allocation grants from the central government (known as DAU) contribute the majority of subnational government revenues, including the Ecological Fiscal Transfers mechanism, which allows for disbursements from provincial to district or city governments. Several provinces have implemented budget tagging, notably for mitigation activities. Future challenges include generating uniform mechanisms and standards for budget tagging at national and subnational levels.

The Ministry of Finance and one of its special mission vehicles (PT SMI) launched SIO—an integrated platform to fund projects associated with the achievement of Sustainable Development Goals (SDGs)—in 2018. SIO is a blended finance instrument designed to combine and channel public and private finance to the various stages of a project's development life cycle. Public funds raised through this platform are expected to overcome obstacles to financing SDG-related projects, and crowd in large amounts of private-sector investment. By March 2022, 35 partners had committed $3.27 billion, and by mid-2023, about $324 million had been disbursed to 97 blended finance projects, comprising 80 project development and 17 financing projects, and 61 ecosystem-enabler activities, including 53 capacity-building, sharing sessions, and business matchmaking, and eight activities related to coordination between state-owned enterprises and university SDG centers. In 2022, the Asian Development Bank approved a $150 million loan to support a green finance facility under SIO to develop and mobilize public and private funds for green and bankable infrastructure projects.

continued on next page

Box 4.2 *continued*

The Government of Indonesia is also developing infrastructure and regulations to support this approach. This includes Disaster Pooling Fund infrastructure, which will integrate the state property asset insurance management, and regulations such as the Ministry of Finance and National Disaster Risk Management disaster budget tracking, risk information strengthening, education, and dissemination requirements. The government's insurance body, *Asuransi Barang Milik Negara*, has begun to insure state assets, such as stadiums and ministry buildings.

As a next step, the government could consider introducing climate resilience-related finance mechanisms into existing public finance mechanisms. It could do this by developing solid criteria for financing eligible investments with resilience bonds, building bond issuer capacity, and adopting, for example, climate resilience principles for issuing green bonds with resilience features in the existing bond-related framework—i.e., green bonds, green sukuk, SDG bonds, state-owned enterprise bonds, and so on.

Key takeaways

- Innovative climate finance instruments are necessary as Indonesia's climate commitments expand, most recently updated under its Enhanced Nationally Determined Contributions and Long-Term Strategy on Low Carbon Development and Climate Resilience 2050. The frameworks help the government close gaps in climate finance needs.
- Optimizing existing tools and instruments related to funding and finance, for example, budget allocations and fiscal transfers, while strengthening the capacity of government stakeholders, the business world, and financial institutions to accelerate climate resilient development.
- Innovative climate instruments can be leveraged at the regional level by encouraging regional governments to implement climate budget tagging systems and ecologically based fiscal transfers linked to central planning and budgeting systems.

Sources: Ministry of Finance, 2018. *Public Finance for Climate Change in Indonesia 2016–2018.*; Ministry of Finance. 2020. Public Finance for Climate Change in Indonesia 2018–2020; Ministry of Finance, 2023. *Green Sukuk Allocation and Impact Report 2019–2023*; Ministry of Finance. *Disaster Risk Financing and Insurance Framework (PARB)*; PT SMI. 2022. Annual Report 2022; PT SMI. 2023. Update on the Implementation of Blended Finance, presented during the 3rd Indonesia Stakeholders Meeting, 21 June 2023; CPI and BKF. 2014. The Landscape of Public Climate Finance in Indonesia Finance; Ministry of Finance. 2021. Enabling Environment for Private Sector Engagement in Climate Change Adaptation Projects. Ministry of Finance. 2021. Enabling Environment for Private Sector Engagement in Climate Change Adaptation Projects.

CFAs can use climate-related risk information to prioritize adaptation interventions to ensure efficient use of public resources (Bellon and Massetti 2022b; GCA 2019). They can also use risk information to assess the risk reduction potential of investments—for example, the public investment rules set up in Bolivia, Costa Rica, and Peru (UNDRR 2019). Notably, public investments in Peru are subject to monitoring and evaluation mechanisms that include considering climate-related risks and adaptations (Office of the Director-General of Public Investment 2016)

Budget Allocation and Revenue Generation

CFAs can incorporate climate-related risk information and scenarios in budgeting to support more effective resource allocation. Climate-related risk information can help them prioritize adaptation and understand which expenditures are at risk (Oxford Policy Management 2021; GCA 2019). Methods are available for integrating this information into budgetary decisions throughout the different stages of the PFM cycle budget—planning, preparation, execution, and control. They include:

- **Signaling adaptation actions in a circular for preparing a budget:** When planning a budget cycle, a report or circular can help signal budgetary actions for adaptation (World Bank 2014). CFAs can use circulars to communicate guidance to ministries—for example, on budget preparation processes, or climate-related assumptions—and to understand sector priorities and targets (Gonguet et al. 2021; Shah et al. 2021). They can use this information when deciding budget allocations. An example is Pakistan's Budget Call Circulars, which require sector ministries to submit forward-looking spending estimates for planning the annual budget cycle (Government of Pakistan 2017).

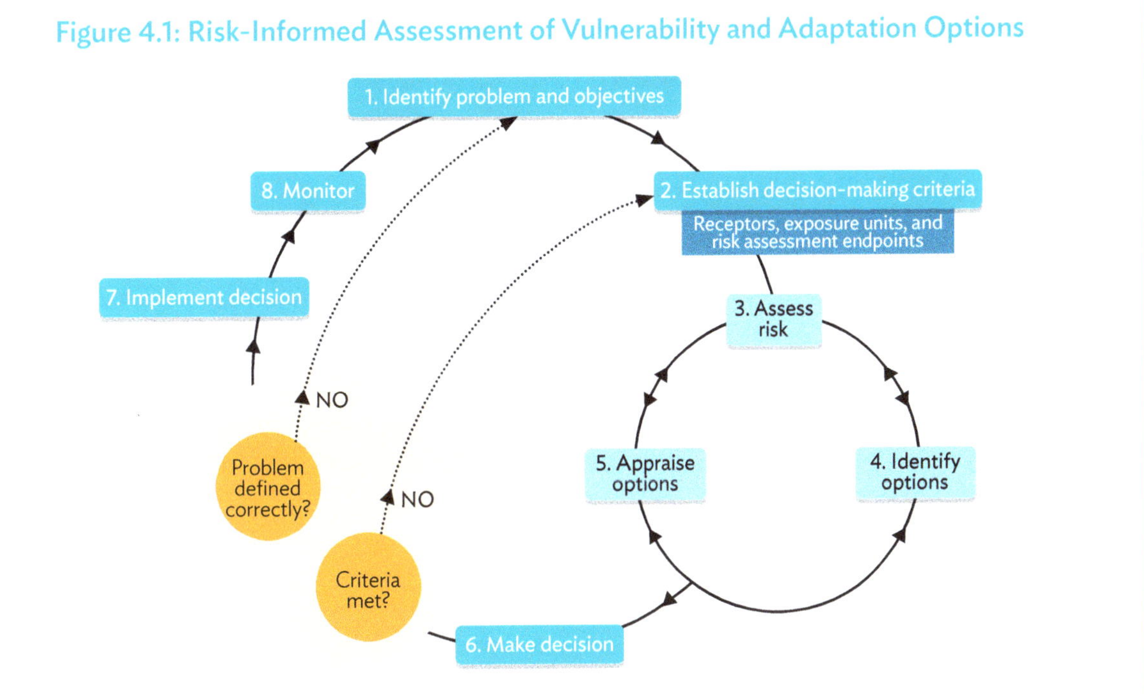

Figure 4.1: Risk-Informed Assessment of Vulnerability and Adaptation Options

Source: Figure 14-2 in Noble, I.R., S. Huq, Y.A. Anokhin, J. Carmin, D. Goudou, F.P. Lansigan, B. Osman-Elasha, and A. Villamizar. 2014: Adaptation Needs and Options. In: *Climate Change 2014: Impacts, Adaptation, and 1473 Vulnerability. Part A: Global and Sectoral Aspects. Contribution of Working Group II to the Fifth 1474 Assessment Report of the Intergovernmental Panel on Climate Change* [C.B. et al]. Cambridge, UK and New York: Cambridge University Press. https://www.ipcc.ch/site/assets/uploads/2018/02/WGIIAR5-FrontMatterA_FINAL.pdf.

- **Incorporating climate-related risk information and scenarios into long-term budgets:** In the PFM cycle's budget preparation stage, it is possible to incorporate adaptation and climate-related risk information in long-term processes (World Bank 2014). For example, countries can use climate-related risk scenarios to inform medium-term expenditure ceilings in aggregate and for different sectors, which guides budget allocations (Shah et al. 2021). India and Nepal do this since their budget allocations and expenditure ceilings for the forestry and water management sectors contain adaptation components (Shah et al. 2021). Long-term budgeting frameworks can give a government a better view of likely recurring expenses, allowing it to accommodate uncertainty by adjusting allocations as needs and requirements change (World Bank 2014).

- **Tracking and tagging adaptation expenditure:** Throughout the preparation, execution, and control stages of the PFM cycle, CFAs can track and monitor adaptation expenditure (Gonguet et al. 2021). They can use a ***climate change public expenditure and institutional review*** to assess the effectiveness of spending on adaptation and use this information to allocate resources efficiently and identify existing funding gaps, creating an understanding of how to approach uncertainty in budgetary processes (World Bank 2014). ***Climate budget tagging*** can help CFAs identify and track expenditure on climate change priorities such as adaptation, developing a methodology for defining and identifying budget expenditure that is relevant for climate change. Although budget tagging system objectives and design might differ across countries, common objectives include mobilizing climate change-related funding and identifying financing gaps. Successful budget tagging incorporates the tagging methodology across the budget cycle, uses definitions consistently across government, and aligns the methodology with national strategies and policies (World Bank 2021a). For example, local governments can use performance-based climate resilience grants to integrate adaptation and resilience in local development planning. Central governments allocate these grants through their regular budget cycle and track the funds through performance assessments that provide transparency on resource use and effectiveness (UNCDF 2018).

- **Integrating PFM:** To mitigate the risk of creating inefficiencies, CFAs can mainstream adaptation and other climate change considerations into existing PFM processes rather than create new frameworks (Gonguet et al. 2021). Countries can leverage existing strengths in the PFM framework and adjust the approach for incorporating adaptation based on country-specific circumstances (Shah et al. 2021).

Investment Prioritization

CFAs can use project appraisal tools to prioritize adaptation investments and assess the potential for reducing risks. Appraisal of proposed adaptation investments can be an important step in the budgeting stage of the PFM cycle and help CFAs prioritize adaptation investments. Armenia's approach to climate-smart public investment management is a strong example (Box 4.3).

Box 4.3: Climate-Smart Public Investment Management: Lessons from Armenia

Armenia's public investment management (PIM) Decree[a] prescribes the use of multicriteria analysis to prioritize public investment projects with projected costs greater than 1 billion Armenian Dram (AMD; about $2.6 million), at the same time this threshold is set AMD3 billion or $7.7 million in the first year of implementation. Lower-cost projects do not require multicriteria project appraisal and go through the general budgeting framework for approval by the relevant government agency. Regardless of the approval route, all approved projects are included in the medium-term expenditure framework and annual budget.

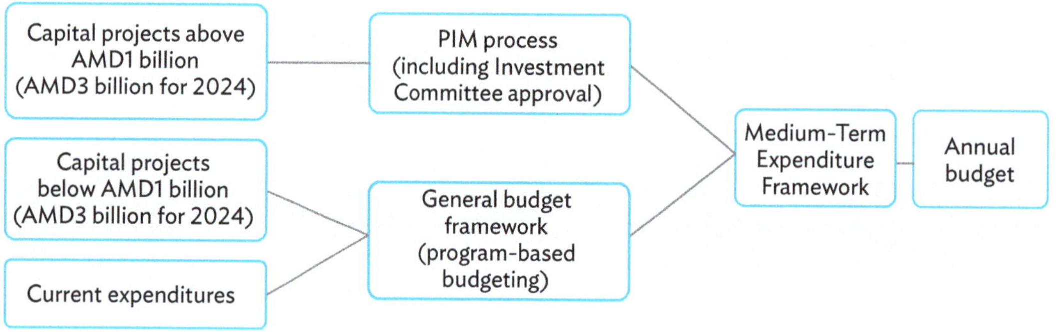

The PIM decree project approval process is as follows. Public agencies prepare investment proposals, facilitated by guidance materials included in the annex to the PIM decree, and submit them to the Ministry of Economy for initial assessment. This ministry forwards prioritized projects to the Ministry of Finance, which assesses funding needs relative to fiscal space. The Investment Committee—headed by the prime minister, and including key ministers and one independent, nonvoting expert—makes the final decision, based on advice from the two ministries.

The decree defines public investment projects as those carried out at the expense of the consolidated budget, including financial resources provided through international credit or grant agreements. Periodic costs that aim to maintain the current state of an asset or replace an existing depreciated asset are not subject to this regulation. This means that the PIM decree applies to capital projects unless they are replacing existing assets.

continued on next page

Box 4.3 *continued*

Six evaluation criteria are used for public investment projects:

1. Impact on human capital.
2. Public importance of the infrastructure, including urgency and necessity.
3. Extent of compliance with the sector strategy.
4. Impact on climate change.
5. Project risk, including exposure to climate and disaster risks, and risk management approach.
6. Economic internal rate of return.

It is important to note that the original decree did not include impact on climate change (criterion 4) or define project risk (criterion 5) in terms of exposure to climate and disaster risks. These criteria were updated on 9 February 2023. All criteria are scored on a scale of 0–3 except for criteria 4 (Impact on climate change), which is scored on a scale 0-2. The projects with total higher scores have higher chances to be approved for funding by the Investment Committee. For example, under criterion 4 (impact on climate change), a project or program would score:

- 2 points if it contributes to reducing greenhouse gas emissions, including carbon dioxide.
- 1 point if it does not contribute to reducing or increasing greenhouse gas emissions, including carbon dioxide.
- 0 points if it contributes to increasing greenhouse gas emissions, including carbon dioxide, or there is no information on the sample form, preliminary feasibility study, or feasibility study.

Criterion 4 does not include adaptation, but the broader definition of project risk (criterion 5) in terms of exposure to climate and disaster risks and risk management approach implies that all investments that are subject to the PIM decree need to demonstrate that they facilitate adaptation to climate change risk, or, at minimum, are designed with climate proofing in mind.

The PIM decree represents an important part of the budgeting stage of the public financial management cycle. The February 2023 update means that it also functions as a project appraisal tool to prioritize adaptation investments and assess climate risk reduction potential.

Armenia is developing further guidance and adaptation plans. Under an Asian Development Bank policy-based loan, the country is preparing further guidance to support comprehensive adoption and implementation of the PIM decree, specifically on how to incorporate climate adaptation into investment decisions. At the same time, under separate technical assistance Asian Development Bank is developing an agriculture sector adaptation investment plan to support Armenia's agriculture strategy. The investment plan will demonstrate compliance with PIM decree criteria, making a strong economic case for investing in climate adaptation in the sector.

Key takeaways

- The first adoption of project prioritization approach and methods may be challenging, so a gradual implementation is critical for the initiative to succeed. In Armenia's case, the government initially defined higher cost threshold for projects to be assessed by the PIM decree to have fewer projects to be processed with PIM methodology. This was done to test the methodology and build capacity to be able to process a larger number of projects.
- The multicriteria analysis approach may include explicit criteria showing linkages to sector strategies, climate change mitigation impacts, and climate-related risk resilience.
- Good practice in the project prioritization methodology is crucial. However, equally important is guidance and practice of application of the methodology in the context of evaluating adaptation investments. Solid assessment requires that the implementing agency has skills, knowledge, and capacity.

Source: Decree N 175 of Government of Republic of Armenia "on approving the procedure for revealing, developing, appraisal and determining priorities of public investment projects" issued on 9 February 2023. https://www.arlis.am/documentview.aspx?docid=174111 .

Appraisal Tools for Prioritizing Investments

CFAs can use various appraisal tools to prioritize projects to ensure that public spending is effective and efficient. To select the most effective investment, within or across sectors, geographies, and time frames, different approaches may be suitable, depending on government capacity and assessment criteria (Climate Adapt 2022a).

Cost–benefit analysis (CBA) can help CFAs understand the economic outcomes and wider social implications of an investment (FAO 2018). CBA can be accompanied by distributional impact analysis to consider the impacts for different stakeholders (Bellon and Massetti 2022a). CBA is commonly used to evaluate and prioritize adaptation investments—for example, selecting adaptation solutions for coffee production in Uganda (FAO 2018) and prioritizing flood and erosion management options in the UK (Box 4.4; UNFCCC 2011). It can also be useful for improving the effectiveness of adaptation spending. That said, the analysis can be complicated and requires significant amounts of data.

Cost-effectiveness analysis assesses the effectiveness of adaptation options in achieving specific, predefined targets (Van Ierland, de Bruin, and Watkiss 2013). For example, alternative adaptation investments could assess the flood risk reduction potential of every dollar spent. Unlike CBA, cost-effectiveness analysis does not require the benefits of an investment to be measured in monetary terms and can be an alternative approach for identifying adaptation options that achieve an acceptable level of resilience at the lowest cost (Climate Adapt 2022b). As an example, vulnerable communities in Small Island Development States in the Pacific have used this approach to assess the effectiveness of adaptation options to ensure they can access water resources as part of a capacity-building project (UNFCCC 2011).

Box 4.4: Cost–Benefit Analysis to Identify Priority Adaptation Investments: Lessons from the United Kingdom

The United Kingdom (UK) is experiencing increasing costs and damages from flood risks. In England alone, 1.5 million people are exposed to a high risk of annual flooding, which causes $350 million in damages to residential properties each year. Assuming no population growth, the number of exposed people is estimated to increase to 1.7 million–2.2 million by 2050 and could increase the cost of damage to residential properties by 78%.

With increased risk of flooding, the UK is likely to need to scale up adaptation expenditure. The country already has a strong focus on building flood resilience, spending the equivalent of more than $1 billion on flood alleviation schemes in 2021, including building flood and coastal infrastructure defenses, improving access to insurance cover, strengthening land and building regulations, and mapping surface water flooding. Although this is estimated to mitigate as much as 50% of future damage costs, further adaptation finance will be required from public and private sources to reduce the impacts of outstanding exposures.

Local authorities are using cost-benefit analysis (CBA) approaches to prioritize adaptation investments. The UK Government's flood and coastal erosion risk management action plan provides a framework to guide decision-making and operationalize adaptations for ministries, government institutions, local authorities, and private sector organizations. Since 2015, the government has worked on 700 projects with local authorities to improve flood resilience in over 300,000 homes. This guidance recommends a CBA framework to prioritize adaptation actions that can deliver resilience at the lowest cost.

In 2009, CBA was used to appraise options for flood and coastal defenses in the northeast England town of Redcar. Options ranged from no further action to a managed adaptive approach to assess different levels of improvement. The analysis found that, for severe flood risks with return periods of 100 years or more, a managed adaptive approach for improving seawalls and erosion prevention infrastructure could have five times more economic benefit than costs, and the local authority has since adopted this approach to build a new seawall and fund maintenance of other resilient infrastructure, with estimated benefits reaching more than $176 million in 2013.

continued on next page

Box 4.4 *continued*

Although the CBA approach allows local authorities to identify the most cost-efficient adaptation options, it can be data-intensive. The Redcar CBA used coastal flood modeling to estimate current and future flood risks, and data from contractors and cost databases to estimate the costs of adaptation investments, including replacing end-of-life items, constructing new seawalls, and maintenance work. The analysis appraised the benefits of adaptation in terms of avoided damages. However, CBAs have limitations in capturing changing risks, as they are typically carried out only once. Monitoring and evaluation is therefore important for assessing whether actions are performing as expected, if further investment is needed in response to changing risks, and to improve the robustness of ongoing analyses.

Key takeaways

- CBA can allow governments to manage budgets effectively by prioritizing cost-effective actions.
- In some cases, CBA approaches can reveal no-regret investments where benefits significantly outstrip costs.
- CBA may not be suitable where infrastructure costs are high and risks are more uncertain. In these cases, more adaptive approaches to investment may be required.

Sources: Climate Change Committee. 2019. *Progress in Preparing for Climate Change*; Climate Change Committee. 2021. *Progress in Preparing for Climate Change*; Defra. 2010. *Coastal Schemes with Multiple Funders and Objectives FD2635: Case Study Report 12 Redcar Flood Alleviation Scheme*; Sayers, P. B., M. S. Horritt, E. Penning-Rowsell, and A. Mckenzie, A. 2015. *Climate Change Risk Assessment 2017: Projections of future flood risk in the UK*. London: Sayers and Partners; UNFCCC. 2011. *Assessing the Costs and Benefits of Adaptation Options—An Overview of Approaches*. Bonn: United Nations Climate Change Secretariat.

CFAs can use multicriteria assessments (MCAs) to understand the impacts of different adaptation investment options against a broad range of criteria. By looking at social, environmental, technical, and economic criteria, MCAs allow CFAs to understand the tradeoffs and synergies between objectives (Chambwera et al. 2014; UNFCCC 2011). The Philippines case study in Box 4.1, while not an example of direct use of MCA, demonstrates how qualitative and quantitative criteria can be built into adaptation spending decisions to align with nationally identified priorities.

Finally, CFAs can use climate-related risk narratives to communicate climate-related risk information and highlight uncertainty around future climate-related risks. Use of such narratives can build capacity to integrate climate-related risk information into decision-making and help CFAs identify adaptation and resilience options that are suitable to a specific location (Jack and Jones 2019).

Accounting for Uncertainty

Where significant uncertainty surrounds future climate-related risks and their impacts, several dynamic approaches can help make funding decisions easier. Public investment decisions made today can be for long-lived infrastructure and therefore need to account for climatic conditions decades into the future. Adaptation investments are often costly and may only be cost-effective under high physical risk scenarios. Public adaptation investment should therefore be an iterative process that is updated as climate-related risks evolve and become better understood (Noble et al. 2014). Using such adaptive pathways and scenario-based analysis can help CFAs account for uncertainty.

Uncertainties around climate-related risks can lead to challenges when planning adaptation investments and creates a risk for potential maladaptation (ADB 2022). Dynamic adaptive pathways can enable CFAs to adapt to changing circumstances over time, by outlining sequences of policy actions. The approach allows them to prioritize smaller or less risky actions early on and lay out a range of options for different future scenarios (ADB 2022). This allows them to re-evaluate strategies over time and gives them flexibility to adapt investment strategies as needs and priorities change (ADB 2022).

Using scenario-based analysis—also known as non-probabilistic assessment methodologies—allows CFAs to include uncertainties over climate-related risks when assessing the effectiveness of potential investments (Chambwera et al. 2014). This methodology is suitable when the probability that a specific climate scenario will happen is highly uncertain (Chambwera et al. 2014). One type of scenario-based analysis uses Representative Concentration Pathways, the widely used approach to model impacts of climate-related risks that was discussed in Box 2.3.

Approaches to Mobilizing Private and International Adaptation Finance

Private and international finance are likely to be important for meeting adaptation financing needs, as the public sector alone is unlikely to meet the scale of resource mobilization required. Competition and innovation in the private sector and the availability of concessional climate finance can also make private finance more efficient in some cases. Additional adaptation finance from the private sector and international sources is therefore necessary, especially in developing countries with limited fiscal space (Bellon and Massetti 2022a). Beyond financing, private sector adaptation is also important for increasing the physical resilience of the economy (Crawford and Church 2019; Tall et al. 2021).

CFAs can help coordinate private and international finance for adaptation and resilience. Barriers to private investment in adaptation, such as technology risks and information asymmetry, can lead to a lower-than-efficient level of private action on adaptation (CDKN 2013; Bellon and Massetti 2022a). Adaptation to climate risks often requires large-scale infrastructure investments—for example, to protect against rising sea levels or to build resilient transportation networks. Because the market does not compensate the private sector accurately enough for these goods, government intervention is necessary to ensure sufficient provision (CDKN 2013). CFAs can help coordinate private actors' responses to ensure that investors capture the full benefits and returns of their investment and the country achieves a sufficient level of adaptation (Bellon and Massetti 2022a).

From a fiscal perspective, the funding of adaptation investments is an important consideration. The distinction between *funding* (meeting lifetime costs) and *financing* (meeting immediate upfront costs) determines the impact of an investment on a country's fiscal health (Institute for Government 2017). If a project is financed by private sector investors, but still funded by the public sector, then there is no benefit to fiscal health. To reduce the amount of public funding for climate-related risk adaptation, CFAs can focus on identifying adaptation projects that the private sector can fund.

CFAs can use fiscal policy and regulations to make it easier for businesses to get financing and reduce investment risks, encouraging the private sector to fund adaptation projects in new sectors and markets (Crawford and Church 2019; Bellon and Massetti 2022a). Actions include: developing long-term plans for action on adaptation to climate-related risks, designing and implementing instruments targeted at incentivizing private adaptation investment and financing, improving access to financial services, and facilitating access to international sources of adaptation finance.

Incorporating adaptation into long-term development plans can create a credible vision on adaptation and anchor investor expectations. Long-term adaptation plans—including for nationally determined contributions, long-term strategies, or national adaptation plans (NAPs)—can incentivize private sector investment in adaptation (Tall et al. 2021). Credible long-term plans help the private sector identify adaptation priorities and needs, provide access to climate-related risk information, and signal government commitment to action on adaptation (Tall et al. 2021). For example, priorities specified in Uganda's NAP align with private bank products targeting support for private sector activities that support national adaptation priorities (IISD 2017), while Thailand used climate risk analysis as a scientific foundation to align its NAP priorities with strategy development and subnational planning (Box 4.5).

Box 4.5: Climate Risk Analysis for National Adaptation Plans: Lessons from Thailand

Although Thailand is vulnerable to climate-related risks, lack awareness of specific risks extends particularly to the local level. Thailand is ranked as the world's 10th most climate-affected country, and is projected to experience more variable precipitation patterns and more frequent floods and droughts. Although adaptation to climate-related risks has already been incorporated into national strategies and frameworks, provincial and municipal authorities lack information on climate risks and vulnerabilities. To close this gap, Thailand started developing a climate risk-informed national adaptation plan (NAP) in 2015.

NAPs can help governments align adaptation priorities with strategy development. They aim to help countries improve their resilience to climate-related risks and mainstream adaptation in their wider policies, programs, and strategies.

Thailand's NAP covers six sectors: water management, public health, tourism, agriculture and food security, natural resource management, and human settlements. Thailand has included the priorities identified in the NAP in national strategies and subnational planning, and aligned financing tools and budgeting systems with the adaptation requirements outlined in the NAP. Objectives of the NAP include building resilience to climate-related risks, mainstreaming adaptation in policy, increasing awareness of climate-related risk adaptation, and improving stakeholder adaptation readiness.

Climate risk analysis provides a scientific foundation for Thailand's NAP, which identifies and prioritizes actions on adaptation based on national climate risks. It uses analysis that identifies localized climate risks to develop risk maps that will highlight adaptation gaps and needs. This approach demonstrates good practice by using a risk-informed evidence base to match adaptation interventions to the most urgent needs. The government will communicate risks specific to sectors and locations to stakeholders to help them build resilience, establish early warning systems, and prioritize interventions.

The analyses underpinning the NAP are mainstreamed in development strategies, which has created coherence across strategies. Thailand has also integrated the climate-related risk analysis at the heart of the NAP into sector development strategies and regional plans, contributing to a consistent use of climate-related risk information. The NAP development process included estimates of implementation costs, informing budgeting and financing instrument analysis.

Collaboration with national stakeholders and international organizations is a vital aspect of the NAP's development and contributes to capacity building. The government developed the NAP with the German Agency for International Cooperation (GIZ) between 2015 and 2021. Assistance from international organizations and collaboration with local stakeholders from focus sectors also helped create an understanding of regional climate-related risks. The analysis and stakeholder engagement raised awareness among relevant departments and helped improve technical capacity.

Key takeaways

- NAPs underpinned by robust and consistent analysis can help governments identify adaptation needs and priorities, and guide their planning and budget allocation.
- Stakeholder engagement can help build technical capacity and awareness of climate-related risks among sector and regional agencies.

Sources: Climate Change Management and Coordination Division. n.d. *Thailand's National Adaptation Plan*. Bangkok, Thailand: Ministry of Natural Resources and Environment; GIZ. 2020. *Climate risk prevention: Thailand's National Adaptation Plan*. https://www.giz.de/en/worldwide/94024.html; NAP Global Network. 2019. *Thailand National Adaptation Plan*. NAP Secretariat; K. Sakhakara. 2017. *Thailand's National Adaptation Plan (NAP) Process Presentation*. Bangkok, Thailand: Climate Change Coordination and Management Division; Songkhao, C. n.d. *The 1st Draft of Thailand National Adaptation Plan Presentation*. Climate Change Coordination and Management Division; UNFCC LDC Expert Group. 2021. *National Adaptation Plans 2020: Progress in the Formulation and Implementation of NAPs*. Bonn: United Nations Climate Change Secretariat.

Developing a financing strategy to complement adaptation plans provides additional communication on adaptation investment needs. As well as communicating needs to the private sector, a financing strategy can provide transparency about public resource allocation (IDB 2021). It can also help price climate-related risks correctly, and so mitigate the issue of private underinvestment in adaptation (Tall et al. 2021).

CFAs can leverage the private sector by creating financing instruments and taking actions that lower risks and increase incentives to get involved in adaptation investments (Tall et al. 2021). High investment risks can reduce returns on investments or decrease access to financing, and so reduce the incentives to invest, for example, in new adaptation technologies (One Planet Lab 2021). Blended finance—a combination of concessional and private finance—can reduce risks to the private sector of investing in emerging technologies or markets (One Planet Lab 2021). For example, the Acumen Resilient Agriculture Fund (ARAF) provides blended finance to draw investors to new technologies that increase resilience to climate-related risks among smallholder farmers in Africa (Acumen 2021). Guarantees can also reduce the risks associated with an investment by compensating investors for any losses (Richmond et al. 2020).

By sharing risks with the public sector, PPPs encourage private sector engagement in adaptation and are particularly beneficial for large-scale infrastructure projects (IISD 2017; Tall et al. 2021). CFAs can identify suitable PPP projects through a long-term adaptation plan that prioritizes adaptation interventions (World Bank 2021b). Examples of successful PPPs can be found in Cambodia, for financing climate resilient road infrastructure (Tall et al. 2021), and in Ethiopia, for increasing the use of irrigation in agriculture (IISD 2017). Chile's approach to PPP development is illustrated in Box 4.6.

Box 4.6: Mobilizing the Private Sector: Lessons from Chile

Chile's 2019 Financial Strategy on Climate Change outlines a plan to finance climate objectives. The country developed the strategy to meet its Nationally Determined Contribution objectives and direct resources toward building a resilient, low-carbon economy. The strategy has three pillars:

1. **Generating and analyzing information and data:** The first pillar is focused on gathering information and analysis to inform the mobilization of capital investments in line with national strategies and priorities. It targets private–public coordination across all sectors to improve the generation, management, and disclosure of information on climate-related risks and opportunities.

2. **Developing financial instruments and markets:** The second pillar is focused on the design and implementation of financial and economic instruments and how they can help achieve a resilient low-carbon economy. It aims to promote collaboration between sectors and engage the private sector to design innovative green financial instruments.

3. **Strengthening the finance sector:** The third pillar is focused on enhancing understanding, capabilities, and action on climate-related risks and opportunities in the finance sector. It aims to bring down barriers to resource mobilization, such as a lack of understanding of climate-related risks and opportunities, by promoting and generating technical knowledge on physical climate-related risks transition opportunities.

Chile's financing strategy is an example of good practice for engaging the private sector in climate financing and investment. Built around public–private sector coordination, it aims to mobilize private sector resources by improving public and private knowledge on the economic implications of climate-related risks and developing good practice climate policies to improve the investment environment. Between 2019 and 2021, the Ministry of Finance issued more than $7 billion in sovereign green bonds at low interest rates to public and private actors that were embarking on green projects. This green bond financed a major project developing an electric bus mobility network across the country. The Ministry of Finance took a role in redesigning the regulatory frameworks around asset ownership and operation, allowing private sector fleet providers and bus operators to develop a public–private partnership with the transport authority, enabling it to purchase new e-buses for lease to fleet providers.

To strengthen its strategy further, Chile could increase the use of information and data to direct private sector capital to priority adaptation areas. The Ministry of Finance is developing a 'green taxonomy' setting out financing criteria for climate adaptation and mitigation activities, which recommends financing mechanisms suitable for different solutions to act as a green financing roadmap. However, the initiative largely focuses on financing mechanisms for mitigation and has limited recommendations for adaptation. Directing the focus on adaptation measures and relevant financial instruments could help scale up adaptation finance that meets Chile's resilience needs.

continued on next page

Box 4.6 *continued*

Key takeaways

- Improving the enabling environment for private sector engagement can successfully attract and enable private investment.
- Engaging with the private sector to understand barriers to investment can help develop successful partnerships.
- Using climate-related risk information to target priority adaptation actions can help build resilience in the areas of greatest need.

Sources: Jaramilo, M. and T. Lecaros. 2019. *How Chile's New Finance Strategy Can Support It Achieve Carbon Neutrality.* https://blogs.iadb.org/sostenibilidad/en/how-chiles-new-finance-strategy-can-support-it-achieve-carbon-neutrality/; Ministerio de Hacienda. 2022. *Estrategia Financiera Frente al Cambio Climático* (Ministry of Finance. 2022. *Financial Strategy on Climate Change*); Ministry of Finance. 2019. *Chile: Financial Strategy on Climate Change.* Government of Chile.

Actions targeting improved financial inclusion can help increase private sector participation in adaptation and resilience. CFAs can use fiscal policy to improve access to financial services—such as savings accounts, borrowing and insurance—that can be important for increasing private sector action on adaptation (Bellon and Massetti 2022a). An example is the 2015 Financial Inclusion Strategy in Pakistan, where a target for 50% of the adult population to access formal financial services by 2020 focused on increasing financial service access points, promoting digital transactions, improving provider capacity, and raising financial awareness (World Bank 2016).

Access to international climate finance can provide additional funding for adaptation. CFAs can leverage international climate finance to provide lower-cost financing for adaptation projects, such as improving climate finance readiness and establishing green and blue bond markets.

To enhance climate finance readiness, CFAs can facilitate access to international climate finance by targeting improvements in project and program formulation, project implementation, and the monitoring of international climate finance flows (UNDP 2012). They can also help identify projects suitable for private investment and match them with investors (Tall et al. 2021). For example, the UK-funded Climate Finance Accelerator helps middle-income households secure financing for their climate activities and connects them with private investors (BEIS 2022).

Establishing green and blue bond markets can provide financing for adaptation investments and connect projects with investors (Tall et al. 2021).[7] Indonesia's green bond market was established in 2017 and the Seychelles established the world's first blue bonds market in 2018. Both will use the proceeds to expand marine protected areas and develop a blue economy (World Bank 2018; World Bank n.d.). CFAs can facilitate the growth of both bond markets by identifying and selecting suitable projects, assets, and expenditures for inclusion, and in developing a bond issuance framework (ADB 2021).

---

[7] In general, green bonds support climate change adaptation and mitigation, and blue bonds target investments in the marine, coastal, and fisheries sectors (ADB 2021).

Key Resources for Central Finance Agency Stakeholders

Budgeting for Climate Change: A Guidance Note for Governments to Integrate Climate Change into Budgeting (Shah et al. 2021): This guidance builds on experiences of climate budgeting from the Asia and Pacific region and highlights successful budgeting processes that address climate risk. The report offers CFAs detailed guidance on the integration of climate in PFM processes.

Economic Principles for Integrating Adaptation to Climate Change into Fiscal Policy (IMF 2022): This report looks at the economic rationale for integrating adaptation in fiscal policy.

Enabling Private Investment in Climate Adaptation and Resilience: Current Status, Barriers to Investment and Blueprint for Action (Tall et al. 2021): This report identifies barriers to private sector involvement in climate adaptation and resilience and actions to facilitate better engagement.

Planning and Mainstreaming Adaptation to Climate Change in Fiscal Policy (Bellon and Massetti 2022): This paper provides clear step-by-step guidance for planning and implementing adaptation into fiscal policy that allows for clear monitoring of progression.

Risk-Informed Development: A Strategy Tool for Integrating Disaster Risk Reduction and Climate Change Adaptation into Development (UNDP 2020): This tool provides practical guidance on how to integrate disaster and climate-related risks into development planning to help mainstream climate change adaptation and disaster reduction and facilitate collaborative policymaking.

Toolkit for Engaging the Private Sector in National Adaptation Plans: Supplement to the UNFCCC Technical Guidelines for the NAP Process (IISD 2020): This toolkit supports the engagement of the private sector in NAP development, providing user-friendly technical guidance for government officials on decisive steps for engaging private sector actors throughout the process, addressing gaps, preparations, implementations, and reporting mechanisms.

Glossary of Terms

Central finance agency	The ministry responsible for developing, implementing, and overseeing core national fiscal policies. Although this role is filled by the ministry of finance in most countries, it can also be taken by other agencies, such as the central bank, or by a group of ministries and agencies. This report highlights the role of ministries of planning or economic development in shaping such policies.
Climate impact assessment	An assessment that identifies the risks and opportunities arising from climate change, covering both chronic and acute physical risks.
Climate-related risks	Changes in the severity and frequency of chronic and acute physical hazards caused by global climate change. This report does not consider climate-related transition risks from the transition to a low-carbon economy.
Direct impacts	Impacts of climate-related risks on government expenditures—such as relief payment to affected populations and spending on infrastructure repair, or loss of revenues due to business interruptions or reduction in the tax base. Impacts include: implicit or explicit liabilities from affected state-owned enterprises or public–private partnerships; implicit liabilities from bank failures; and changes to regulations that place additional pressure on requirements from public resources.
Fiscal health	The current state of a government's budget and its ability to meet financial and service obligations.
Fiscal sustainability	A government's ability to maintain expected levels of revenue and expenditures over time.
Indirect impacts	The impacts of climate-related risks on the wider economy and knock-on implications for socioeconomic and fiscal outcomes, including: short-term impacts on economic output and public services; and longer-term impacts of increased poverty and reduced investment resources.

References

Acumen. 2021. Acumen Resilient Agriculture Fund: Investing in Smallholder Farmers. *Blog*, 4 August. https://acumen.org/blog/resilient-agriculture-fund/.

Asian Development Bank (ADB). 2021. *Detailed Guidance for Issuing Green Bonds in Developing Countries.* Manila.

ADB. 2022. *Disaster-Resilient Infrastructure: Unlocking Opportunities for Asia and the Pacific.* Manila.

ADB and World Bank. 2021. *Climate Risk Country Profile: Pakistan.* Manila and Washington, DC.

Adrian, T., J. Morsink, and L.B. Schumacher. 2020a. *Stress Testing at the IMF.* Washington DC: International Monetary Fund.

———. 2020b. Assessing Climate-Change Risk by Stress Testing for Financial Resilience. *IMF Blog*, 5 February. https://blogs.imf.org/2020/02/05/assessing-climate-change-risk-by-stress-testing-for-financial-resilience/.

Aligishiev Z., E. Massetti, and M. Bellon. 2022. Macro-Fiscal Implications of Adaptation to Climate Change. *IMF Staff Climate Notes* 2022/002. Washington, DC: International Monetary Fund.

Allan, S., A. V. Bahadur, S. Venkatramani, and V. Soundarajan. 2019. *The Role of Domestic Budgets in Financing Climate Change Adaptation.* Rotterdam and Washington, DC: Global Commission on Adaptation.

Allen, R., Y. Hurcan, M. Queyranne, and S. Ylaoutinen. 2015. The Evolving Functions and Organization of Finance Ministries. *IMF Working Paper,* 15/232. Washington, DC.: International Monetary Fund.

Amirali, A. 2020. *Financing for Climate Adaptation—An Overview of Current Regimes.* Brighton, UK: Institute of Development Studies.

Artemis. The Artemis Catastrophe Bond and Insurance-linked Securities Deal Directory. https://www.artemis.bm/deal-directory/ibrd-car-123-124/.

Bachmair, F.F. 2016. *Contingent Liabilities Risk Management: A Credit Risk Analysis Framework for Sovereign Guarantees and On-Lending.* Washington, DC: World Bank.

Basel Committee on Banking Supervision. 2021. *Climate-Related Financial Risks— Measurement Methodologies.* Basel.

Department for Business, Energy, and Industry Strategy (BEIS). 2022. *Climate Finance Accelerator.* London.

Bellon, M. and E. Massetti. 2022a. Economic Principles for Integrating Adaptation to Climate Change into Fiscal Policy. *IMF Staff Climate Note 2022/001.* Washington, DC.: International Monetary Fund.

———. 2022b. Planning and Mainstreaming Adaptation to Climate Change in Fiscal Policy. *IMF Staff Climate Note* 2022/003. Washington, DC: International Monetary Fund.

Bonasia, R. and S. Lucatello. 2019. Linking Flood Susceptibility Mapping and Governance in Mexico for Flood Mitigation: A Participatory Approach Model. *Atmosphere,* 10(8): 424.

Browning, S. 2023. Flood Re and Household Flood Insurance. *Commons Library Research Briefing* 8751, UK Parliament, London.

Burns, A., C. Jooste, and G. Schwerhoff. 2021. *Climate Modelling for Macroeconomic Policy: A Case Study for Pakistan*. Washington, DC: World Bank.

Cantelmo, A., G. Melina, and C. Papageorgiou. 2019. Macroeconomic Outcomes in Disaster-Prone Countries. *IMF Working Papers* 2019/217. Washington, DC: International Monetary Fund.

Climate Development and Knowledge Network (CDKN). 2013. *Addressing the Barriers to Climate Investment*.

Cevik, S. and G. Huang. 2018. How to Manage the Fiscal Costs of Natural Disasters. *IMF How-To Notes* 18(03). Washington, DC: International Monetary Fund.

M., G. Heal, C. Dubeux, S. Hallegatte, L. Leclerc, A. Markandya, B. A. McCarl, et. al. 2015. Economics of adaptation. In: *Climate Change 2014: Impacts, Adaptation, and Vulnerability. Part A: Global and Sectoral Aspects*. Contribution of Working Group II to the Fifth Assessment Report of the Intergovernmental Panel on Climate Change. C.B. Field, et al. Cambridge, UK and New York: Cambridge University Press. www.ipcc.ch/site/assets/ uploads/2018/02/WGIIAR5-FrontMatterA_FINAL.pdf.

Clarke, D. J. and S. Dercon. 2016. *Dull Disasters? How Planning Ahead Will Make a Difference.* New York: Oxford University Press.

Climate Adapt. 2022a. *Assessing and Selecting Adaptation Options: 4.1 Choosing an Assessment Framework for Adaptation Options*. European Climate Adaptation Platform. https://climate-adapt.eea.europa.eu/ knowledge/tools/urban-ast/step-4-1.

Climate Adapt. 2022b. *Assessing and Selecting Adaptation Options: 4.2 Conducting a Cost–Benefit Analysis of Adaptation Measures*. European Climate Adaptation Platform. https://climate-adapt.eea.europa.eu/ knowledge/tools/urban-ast/step-4-2.

Climate Centre. 2016. *Disaster Preparation Means Forecast-Based Financing, Not Band-Aids.* The Hague, Netherlands. https://www.climatecentre.org/1619/disaster-preparation-means-forecast-based-financing-not-band-aids/.

Climate Change Committee. 2019. *Progress in Preparing for Climate Change*. London.

———. 2021. *Progress in Adapting to Climate Change*. London.

Climate Change Management and Coordination Division. n.d. *Thailand's National Adaptation Plan*. Bangkok, Thailand: Ministry of Natural Resources and Environment.

Coalition of Finance Ministers for Climate Action. 2022. *Driving Climate Action through Economic and Fiscal Policy and Practice*. Washington, DC.

———. 2023. *Strengthening the Role of Ministries of Finance in Driving Climate Action. A Framework and Guide for Ministers and Ministries of Finance.* Washington, DC.

Congressional Research Service. 2021. *A Brief Introduction to the National Flood Insurance Program.* Washington, DC.

Climate Policy Initiative (CPI). 2023. *Global Landscape of Climate Finance 2023* [B. Buchner et al].

Crawford, A. and C. Church. 2019. *Engaging the Private Sector in National Adaptation Planning Processes*. Winnipeg, Canada: International Institute for Sustainable Development.

Dabla-Norris, E., J. Daniel, M. Nozaki, C. Alonso, V. Balasundharam, M. Bellon, C. Chen, D. Corvino, et al. 2021. *Fiscal Policies to Address Climate Change in Asia and the Pacific*. Departmental Paper No 2021/007, Washington, DC: International Monetary Fund.

Department for Environment, Food and Rural Affairs (Defra). 2010. *Coastal Schemes with Multiple Funders and Objectives FD2635: Case Study Report 12 Redcar Flood Alleviation Scheme.* London.

Dellink, R., E. Lanzi, and J. Chateau. 2019. The Sectoral and Regional Economic Consequences of Climate Change to 2060. *Environmental and Resource Economics,* 72(2).

Department of Finance. 2020. *People's Survival Fund Seeks to Find Solution to Climate Crisis.* Government of the Philippines, 25 November. https://www.dof.gov.ph/peoples-survival-fund-seeks-to-find-solution-to-climate-crisis/.

Development Budget Coordination Committee. 2021. *Fiscal Risks Statement.* Manila: Treasury of the Philippines.

Dunz, N. and S. Power. 2021. *Climate-Related Risks for Ministries of Finance: An Overview.* Washington, DC: Coalition of Finance Ministers for Climate Action.

Ebi, K.L., J.J. Hess, and P. Watkiss. 2017. Health Risks and Costs of Climate Variability and Change. In *Injury Prevention and Environmental Health.* 3rd edition. Washington, DC: International Bank for Reconstruction and Development/World Bank.

United Nations Economic Commission for Latin America and the Caribbean (ECLAC). n.d. *Debt for Climate Adaptation Flyer.* Santiago, Chile.

Eguino, H., R. Delgado, and A. Lopes. 2021. Three Areas Where Finance Ministries Can Help Solve the Climate Crisis. *IDB Blog,* 23 August. https://blogs.iadb.org/gestion-fiscal/en/three-areas-where-finance-ministries-can-help-solve-the-climate-crisis/.

Food and Agriculture Organization of the United Nations (FAO). 2018. Cost–Benefit Analysis for Climate Change Adaptation Policies and Investment in the Agriculture Sectors. *Briefing Note,* February.

Group of Twenty (G20) and Organisation for Economic Co-operation and Development (OECD). 2013. *Disaster Risk Assessment and Risk Financing.*

Global Commission on Adaptation (GCA). 2019. *Adapt Now: A Global Call for Leadership on Climate Resilience.* Rotterdam and Washington, DC.

Getliffe E. 2022. Malawi Anticipatory Action: Process Learning on Trigger Development. Learning Report. *Working Paper,* Centre for Disaster Protection, London.

Global Facility for Disaster Reduction and Recovery (GFDRR). 2013. *Post-Disaster Needs Assessment Guidelines and Recovery Planning, Volume A.* Washington, DC.

GFDRR. 2014. *Recovery and Reconstruction Planning the Aftermath of Typhoon Haiyan.* Washington, DC. https://www.gfdrr.org/en/publication/recovery-and-reconstruction-planning-aftermath-typhoon-haiyan.

GFDRR. 2016. *Country Profile: Mexico.* Global Facility for Disaster Reduction and Recovery. Washington, DC.

Global Green Growth Institute (GGGI). 2022. *Support to the Operationalization of the People's Survival Fund.* Seoul. https://gggi.org/project/support-to-the-operationalization-of-the-peoples-survival-fund/.

Gesellschaft für Internationale Zusammenarbeit (GIZ). 2020. *Climate Risk Prevention: Thailand's National Adaptation Plan.* Bonn:. https://www.giz.de/en/worldwide/94024.html.

GIZ. 2021. *Macroeconomic Models for Climate Resilience.* Bonn.

GIZ. 2022. *Supporting Climate Resilient Economic Development in Kazakhstan.* Bonn.

Global Disaster Preparedness Center. 2013. *Local Disaster Risk Reduction and Management Fund*. Washington, DC: American Red Cross and the International Federation Red Cross and Red Crescent Societies.

Gonguet, F., C. Wendling, O. A. Sakrak, and B. Battersby 2021. Climate-Sensitive Management of Public Finances—Green PFM. *IMF Staff Climate Note* 2021/002. Washington, DC: International Monetary Fund.

Government of Lao People's Democratic Republic. 2018. *Post-Disaster Needs Assessment 2018 Floods, Lao PDR*. Vientiane.

Government of Pakistan. 2017. *Pakistan Climate Change Financing Framework: A Road Map to Systemically Mainstream Climate Change into Public Economic and Financial Management*. Islamabad, Pakistan: United Nations Development Programme Pakistan.

Hallegatte, S., J. Rentschler, and J. Rozenberg. 2020. *Adaptation Principles: A Guide for Designing Strategies for Climate Change Adaptation and Resilience*. Washington, DC: World Bank.

HM Treasury. 2022. *The Green Book: 2. Introduction to Appraisal and Evaluation.* London. https://www.gov.uk/government/publications/the-green-book-appraisal-and-evaluation-in-central-governent/the-green-book-2020#introduction-to-appraisal-and-evaluation.

Hunger Safety Net Programme (HSNP). *About HSNP*. Nairobi: Government of Kenya. https://www.hsnp.or.ke/index.php/as/objectives.

Inter-American Development Bank (IDB). 2017. *Assessment of the Effects and Impacts Caused by Hurricane Irma: The Bahamas*. Santiago, Chile.

IDB. 2020. *Barbados to Strengthen its Risk Management of Natural Disasters and Climate Emergencies*. Santiago, Chile. https://www.iadb.org/en/news/barbados-strengthen-its-risk-management-natural-disasters-and-climate-emergencies (accessed 27 July 2022).

IDB. 2021. *Fiscal Policy and Climate Change*. Santiago, Chile.

International Federation of Red Cross and Red Crescent Societies (IFRC). 2021. *Bangladesh: Forecast-based Financing*. Geneva.

International Institute for Applied Systems Analysis (IIASA). 2020. *CATSIM: A Modeling Approach to Improve Financial Disaster Risk Management*. https://previous.iiasa.ac.at/web/home/research/researchPrograms/RISK/CATSIM.en.html.

International Institute for Sustainable Development (IISD). 2017. *Financing National Adaptation Plan Financing National Adaptation Plan Achievement of Nationally Determined Contribution (NDC) Adaptation Goals*. Winnipeg, Canada.

IISD. 2020. *Toolkit for Engaging the Private Sector in National Adaptation Plans: Supplement to the UNFCCC Technical Guidance for the NAP Process*. Winnipeg, Canada.

International Monetary Fund (IMF). 1999. *Guidelines for Public Expenditure Management*. Washington, DC.

IMF. 2001. *Guidelines for Public Debt Management*. Washington, DC.

IMF. 2015. *Fiscal Policy and Long-Term Growth. IMF Policy Paper*, Washington, DC.

IMF. 2016. *Analyzing and Managing Fiscal Risks: Best Practices*. Washington, DC.

IMF. 2018. *Fiscal Policy: How to Manage the Fiscal Costs of Natural Disasters*. Washington, DC.

IMF. 2018. *Fiscal Transparency Handbook*. Washington, DC.

IMF. 2019a. The Economics of Climate. *Finance and Development* 56(4). December.

IMF. 2019b. *Federated States of Micronesia*. Washington, DC.

IMF. 2020a. *Challenges in Forecasting Tax Revenue. Special Series on Fiscal Policies to Respond to COVID-19.* Washington, DC.

IMF. 2020b. *Managing Fiscal Risks Under Fiscal Stress. Special Series on Fiscal Policies to Respond to COVID-19.* Washington, DC.

IMF. 2022a. *Economic Principles for Integrating Adaptation to Climate Change into Fiscal Policy.* Washington, DC.

IMF. 2022b. *Armenia: Technical Report—Quantifying Fiscal Risks from Climate Change.* Washington, DC.

Institute for Government. 2017. *Financing Infrastructure*. London. https://www.instituteforgovernment.org.uk/ explainer/financing-infrastructure.

Intergovernmental Panel on Climate Change (IPCC). 2022: *Climate Change 2022: Impacts, Adaptation and Vulnerability.* Contribution of Working Group II to the Sixth Assessment Report of the Intergovernmental Panel on Climate Change. Cambridge, UK and New York: Cambridge University Press. https://report.ipcc.ch/ ar6/wg2/IPCC_AR6_WGII_FullReport.pdf.

Irwin, T. and T. Mokdad. 2010. *Managing Contingent Liabilities in Public–Private Partnerships: Practice in Australia, Chile, and South Africa.* Washington, DC: World Bank.

Jack, C. and R. Jones. 2019. *Climate Risk Narratives: 'Humble' Science.* Future Resilience for African Cities and Lands Impact Story 4, October.

Jaramilo, M. and T. Lecaros. 2019. How Chile's New Finance Strategy Can Support it Achieve Carbon Neutrality. *IDB Blog,* 12 December. https://blogs.iadb.org/sostenibilidad/en/how-chiles-new-finance-strategy-can-support-it-achieve-carbon-neutrality/.

Kahn, M.E., K. Mohaddes, R. N. C. Ng, M. H. Pesaran, M. Raissi, and J. C. Yang. 2019. Long-Term Macroeconomic Effects of Climate Change: A Cross-country Analysis. *IMF Working Paper,* 19/215. Washington, DC: , International Monetary Fund.

Kalkuhl, M. and L. Wenz. 2020. The Impact of Climate Conditions on Economic Production. Evidence from a Global Panel of Regions. *Journal of Environmental Economics and Management,* 103(C).

Koks, E. and M. Thissen. 2016. A Multiregional Impact Assessment Model for Disaster Analysis. *Economic Systems Research,* 28(4): 429–49.

Lienert, I. 2010. *Optimal Structures for Ministries of Finance.* Public Financial Management *Blog,* 29 March.

Makortoff, K. 2021. Bank of England Warns of Crackdown on Financing Linked to Climate Risk. *The Guardian,* 28 October.

Meenan, C., J. Ward, and R. Muir-Wood. 2019. *Disaster Risk Finance: A Toolkit*. Bonn: Gesellschaft für Internationale Zusammenarbeit (GIZ). https://indexinsuranceforum.org/sites/default/files/Publikationen03_ DRF_ACRI _DINA4_WEB_190617.pdf.

Millennium Institute. 2015. *Promoting Systems Literacy and Dynamic Modeling Tools for Sustainable Development Worldwide.* Washington, DC.

Ministerio de Hacienda. 2022. *Estrategia Financiera Frente al Cambio Climático.* Government of Chile.

Ministry of Finance. 2019. *Chile: Financial Strategy on Climate Change.* Government of Chile.

Mosk, T.C. 2018. *Bank Response to Higher Capital Requirements: Evidence from a Quasi-natural Experiment.* Harvard Law School Forum on Corporate Governance, 24 May.

Mullan, M. and N. Ranger. 2022. Climate Resilient Finance and Investment: Framing Paper. *OECD Environment Working Papers,* 19, Organisation for Economic Co-operation and Development, Paris.

NAP Global Network. 2019. *Thailand National Adaptation Plan.* NAP Secretariat.

Naude, R. and A. Eberhard. 2017. *The South African Renewable Energy IPP Procurement Programme: Review Lessons Learned and Proposals to Reduce Transaction Costs.* April.

National Integrated Climate Change Database Information and Exchange System (NICCDIES). 2022. People's Survival Fund. Manila: Government of the Philippines. https://niccdies.climate.gov.ph/climate-finance/people-survival-fund.

Noble, I.R., S. Huq, Y.A. Anokhin, J. Carmin, D. Goudou, F.P. Lansigan, B. Osman-Elasha, and A. Villamizar. 2014: Adaptation Needs and Options. In: *Climate Change 2014: Impacts, Adaptation, and 1473 Vulnerability. Part A: Global and Sectoral Aspects. Contribution of Working Group II to the Fifth 1474 Assessment Report of the Intergovernmental Panel on Climate Change* [C.B. et al]. Cambridge, UK and New York: Cambridge University Press. https://www.ipcc.ch/site/assets/uploads/2018/02/WGIIAR5-FrontMatterA_FINAL.pdf.

Organisation for Economic Co-operation and Development (OECD). 2013a. *Government at a Glance 2013.* Paris: OECD Publishing.

OECD. 2013b. *Reviews of Risk Management Policies: Mexico 2013.* Paris: OECD Publishing.

OECD. 2015. *Disaster Risk Financing: A Global Survey of Practices and Challenges.* Paris: OECD Publishing.

OECD. 2020. *Common Ground between the Paris Agreement and the Sendai Framework: Climate Change Adaptation and Disaster Risk Reduction.* Paris: OECD Publishing.

OECD. 2021a. *Climate Change and Long-term Fiscal Sustainability.* Paris: OECD Publishing.

OECD. 2021b. *Introductory Note on Integrating Climate into Macroeconomic Modelling: Drawing on the Danish Experience.* Paris: OECD Publishing.

OECD. 2022. *Building Financial Resilience to Climate Impacts. A Framework for Governments to Manage the Risks of Losses and Damages.* Paris: OECD Publishing.

OECD and World Bank. 2019. Chapter 1. Understanding the Economic and Fiscal Impacts of Disasters. In: *Fiscal Resilience to Natural Disasters Lessons from Country Experiences.* Paris: OECD Publishing.

Office of the Director-General of Public Investment. 2016. *General Guidelines for Public Investment Projects.* Government of Peru.

One Planet Lab. 2021. *Blended Finance for Scaling Up Climate and Nature Investments.* London: LSE, Grantham Research Institute on Climate Change and the Environment.

Oxford Policy Management. 2021. *Climate Finance: Mobilising Domestic Budgets and External Funds for Adaptation. Policy Paper,* Oxford, UK.

Public Expenditure and Financial Accountability Secreteriat. n.d.. *What is PEFA?* Washington DC: PEFA Secretariat. https://www.pefa.org/about .

Philippine Institute for Development Studies. 2017. *A Review of Philippine Government Disaster Financing for Recovery and Reconstruction.* Quezon City, Philippines.

Pigato, M.A. (editor). 2019. *Fiscal Policies for Development and Climate Action.* Washington, DC: World Bank Group.

Public–Private Partnership Legal Resource Center (PPPLRC). *Country Profile: South Africa.* Washington, DC: World Bank Group. https://ppp.worldbank.org/public-private-partnership/country-profile-south-africa.

Quintyn, M. and M.W. Taylor. 2004. Should Financial Sector Regulators Be Independent? International Monetary Fund, *Economic Issues*, 32, 8 March.

Republic of Armenia. 2021. *National Adaptation Plan.* https://unfccc.int/sites/default/files/resource/NAP_Armenia.pdf.

Richmond M., C. Meattle, V. Micale, Padraig Oliver, R. Padmanabhi. 2020. A Snapshot of Global Adaptation Investment and Tracking Methods. Climate Policy Initiative.

Sakhakara, K. 2017. *Thailand's National Adaptation Plan (NAP) Process Presentation.* Bangkok, Thailand: Climate Change Coordination and Management Division.

Sayers, P. B., M. S. Horritt, E. Penning-Rowsell, and A. Mckenzie, A. 2015. *Climate Change Risk Assessment 2017: Projections of future flood risk in the UK.* London: Sayers and Partners.

Signer, B. and R. Poulter. 2021. Disaster Risk Insurance: 5 Insights from the Philippines. *World Bank Blogs*, 1 December. https://blogs.worldbank.org/climatechange/disaster-risk-insurance-5-insights-philippines.

Shah, A., M. Asad, T. Meng, S. Markosyan, S. Biswas, and S. Venkatramani. 2021. *Budgeting for Climate Change: A Guidance Note for Governments to Integrate Climate Change into Budgeting.* United Nations Development Programme.

Singh, R. and A. Plekhanov. 2005. How Should Subnational Government Borrowing Be Regulated? Some Cross-Country Empirical Evidence. *IMF Working Paper*, 2005/054, International Monetary Fund, Washington, DC.

Songkhao, C. n.d. *The 1st Draft of Thailand National Adaptation Plan Presentation.* Bangkok, Thailand: Climate Change Coordination and Management Division.

Swain, M. 2014. Crop Insurance for Adaptation to Climate Change in India. *LSE Working Papers*, 61, London School of Economics and Political Science.

Swiss Re Institute. 2021. *The Economics of Climate Change: No Action Not an Option.*

Tall, A., S. Lynagh, C. B. Vecchi, P. Bardouille, F. M. Pino, E. Shabahat, V. Stenek, F. Stewart, S. Power, C. Paladines, P. Neves, and L. Kerr. 2021. *Enabling Private Investment in Climate Adaptation and Resilience: Current Status, Barriers to Investment and Blueprint for Action.* Washington, DC: World Bank.

Tenzing, J.D. 2020. Integrating Social Protection and Climate Change Adaptation: A Review. *WIREs Climate Change*, 11(2).

The White House. 2022. *Briefing Room: Quantifying Risks to the Federal Budget from Climate Change.* Washington, DC. https://www.whitehouse.gov/omb/briefing-room/2022/04/04/quantifying-risks-to-the-federal-budget-from-climate-change/.

The White House. 2023. *Briefing Room: The Importance of Measuring the Fiscal and Economic Costs of Climate Change.* Washington, DC. https://www.whitehouse.gov/omb/briefing-room/2023/03/14/the-importance-of-measuring-the-fiscal-and-economic-costs-of-climate-change/.

Treasury Committee. 2011. *Principles of Tax Policy.* London: The Stationery Office Limited.

United Nations Capital Development Fund (UNCDF). 2018. *Financing Local Adaptation to Climate Change. Experiences with Performance-Based Climate Resilience Grants.* New York.

United Nations Development Programme (UNDP). 2012. *Readiness for Investment.* New York.

UNDP. 2014. Mexico: *Country Case Study: How Law and Regulation Support Disaster Risk Reduction.* New York.

UNDP. 2020. *Risk-Informed Development: A Strategy Tool for Integrating Disaster Risk Reduction and Climate Change Adaptation into Development.* New York.

United Nations Office for Disaster Risk Reduction (UNDRR). 2019. *Global Assessment Report on Disaster Risk Reduction.* Geneva.

UNDRR and GIZ. 2022. *Technical Guidance on Comprehensive Risk Assessment and Planning in the Context of Climate Change.* Geneva: United Nations Office for Disaster Risk Reduction.

United Nations Environment Programme (UNEP). 2023. *Adaptation Gap Report: Underfinanced. Underprepared.* Nairobi.

UNEP. 2022. *Adaptation Gap Report: Too Little, Too Slow: Climate Adaptation Failure Puts World at Risk.* Nairobi.

United Nations Economic and Social Commission for Asia and the Pacific (UNESCAP). 2017. *Disaster Risk Transfer Mechanisms: Issues and Considerations for the Asia-Pacific Region.* Bangkok.

UNFCCC Least Developed Countries Expert Group. 2021. *National Adaptation Plans 2020: Progress in the Formulation and Implementation of NAPs.* Bonn: United Nations Climate Change Secretariat.

UNFCCC. 2011. *Assessing the Costs and Benefits of Adaptation Options—An Overview of Approaches.* Bonn: United Nations Climate Change Secretariat.

US Office of Management and Budget. 2022. *Climate Risk Exposure: An Assessment of the Federal Government's Financial Risks to Climate Change.* Washington, DC.

Van Ierland, E., K. de Bruin, and P. Watkiss. 2013. *Multi-Criteria Analysis: Decision Support.* MEDIATION Project, Wageningen University, Netherlands.

Waithe, K. 2019. *Avoiding a Debt Disaster. IDB Blog,* 10 July. https://blogs.iadb.org/caribbean-dev-trends/en/avoiding-a-debt-disaster/.

Wang, N., G, Shi, and X. Zhou. 2020. To Move or Not to Move: How Farmers Now Living in Flood Storage Areas of China Decide Whether to Move Out or to Stay Put. *Journal of Flood Risk Management,* 13(2).

WITCHMODEL. 2022. Evaluating Climate Change Impacts and Solutions. https://www.witchmodel.org/.

World Meteorological Organization (WMO). 2023. *WMO Global Annual to Decadal Climate Update: Target Years: 2023 and 2023–2027.* Geneva. https://library.wmo.int/idurl/4/66224.

World Bank. 2013. *Building Morocco's Resilience: Inputs for an Integrated Risk Management Strategy.* Washington, DC.

World Bank. 2014. Moving Toward Climate Budgeting. *Policy Note,* Washington, DC.

World Bank. 2015. Understanding El Niño: What Does it Mean for Commodity Markets? *Special Focus,* Washington, DC.

World Bank. 2016. What Will it Take for Pakistan to Achieve Financial Inclusion? *Feature Story,* 8 February.

World Bank. 2017. *Establishing A Fiscal Risk Management Department in the Ministry of Finance of Serbia.* Washington, DC.

World Bank. 2018. *Seychelles Launches World's First Sovereign Blue Bond.* Washington, DC. https://www.worldbank.org/en/news/press-release/2018/10/29/seychelles-launches-worlds-first-sovereign-blue-bond.

World Bank. 2021a. *Climate Change Budget Tagging: A Review of International Experience. Equitable Growth, Finance and Institutions Insights.* Washington, DC.

World Bank. 2021b. *Investment in Disaster Risk Management in Europe Makes Economic Sense.* Washington, DC.

World Bank. 2022. *Macroeconomic Models for Climate Policy Analysis.* Washington, DC.

World Bank. n.d. *First Corporate Green Bond in Indonesia: Supporting Indonesia Efforts to Fight Climate Change.* Washington, DC.

World Bank and GFDRR. 2012. *Mexico Natural Disaster Fund—A Review.* Washington, DC: International Bank for Reconstruction and Development/World Bank.

World Bank and GFDRR. 2015. *Fiscal Disaster Risk Assessment Options for Consideration: Pakistan.* Washington, DC: International Bank for Reconstruction and Development/World Bank.

World Bank and GFDRR. 2016. *Peru: A Comprehensive Strategy for Financial Protection Against Natural Disasters.* Washington, DC: International Bank for Reconstruction and Development/World Bank.

World Resources Institute (WRI). 2022. *6 Big Findings from the IPCC 2022 Report on Climate Impacts, Adaptation and Vulnerability.* Washington, DC. https://www.wri.org/insights/ipcc-report-2022-climate-impacts-adaptation-vulnerability.

Climate Resilient Fiscal Planning
A Review of Global Good Practices

This report shows how adopting good practices around climate-resilient fiscal planning can help decision-makers in Asia and the Pacific ramp up public and private resources to plug the yawning adaptation financing gap. Outlining a three-step framework, the report explains the need to effectively assess the rising impacts of climate change, develop a fiscal risk management strategy, and optimize available resources. It underscores why coherent action hinges on a solid understanding of the impacts of climate change and how central finance agencies can better integrate climate risk into decision-making to lead the drive toward economic resilience.

About the Asian Development Bank

ADB is committed to achieving a prosperous, inclusive, resilient, and sustainable Asia and the Pacific, while sustaining its efforts to eradicate extreme poverty. Established in 1966, it is owned by 68 members —49 from the region. Its main instruments for helping its developing member countries are policy dialogue, loans, equity investments, guarantees, grants, and technical assistance.

ASIAN DEVELOPMENT BANK
6 ADB Avenue, Mandaluyong City
1550 Metro Manila, Philippines
www.adb.org

Printed in the USA
CPSIA information can be obtained
at www.ICGtesting.com
CBHW060029051024
15376CB00025B/1531